YOU'VE GOT SOME NERVE

YOU'VE GOT SOME NERVE

The Battle Back from an Invisible Injury

DERRYEN PLANTE

LIONCREST
PUBLISHING

YOU'VE GOT SOME NERVE
The Battle Back from an Invisible Injury

ISBN 978-1-5445-0930-3 *Hardcover*
978-1-5445-0929-7 *Paperback*
978-1-5445-0928-0 *Ebook*
978-1-5445-0931-0 *Audiobook*

For my loving family.
For those who have sat with me in the darkness;
and for those who are trying to find their way out.
You are not alone.

CONTENTS

INTRODUCTION 9

1. BEST-LAID PLANS 19

2. COURSE CORRECTIONS 29

3. ASSAULT AND AFTERMATH 79

4. INVISIBLE INJURY 95

5. GETTING HELP 115

6. POST-SURGERY IDENTITY 149

7. GIVING HELP 171

CONCLUSION 185

ACKNOWLEDGMENTS 201

ABOUT THE AUTHOR 205

INTRODUCTION

With my college textbook tucked into my floral-print backpack and coffee in hand, I clocked in to begin another long evening shift. Unlike many women my age, I wasn't heading to an office to answer phones, or to a classroom to teach bright-eyed students; I worked in a prison.

That may sound grim for a twenty-three-year-old woman, but it was all part of my plan. Working at the jail allowed me to work within the criminal justice system and gain valuable firsthand experience, and it provided me with the financial resources to pursue a graduate education. I hoped that each of these aspects would help me progress toward landing my dream job as an investigator for a federal law enforcement agency. It was just one more checkmark on the long list I've been working through since I started watching *Cold Case Files* as a child.

High school honors, check.

Martial arts training, check.

College honors, check.

Law enforcement internships, check.

Graduate studies, underway.

It was Saturday night and everything seemed normal on the unit—or as normal as it ever was. We didn't really do normal; we did controlled chaos. I spent most of my evenings working with juveniles who were classified to the "high risk" unit, which meant I worked with some of the most dangerous juveniles in the entire state.

Don't let the term "juvenile" fool you. Their crimes ran the gamut of felony drug charges to armed robbery, aggravated assault, and attempted murder, to name a few. There was nothing that happened in an adult facility that didn't take place in this facility, especially in my unit. As much as people outside these prison walls believed that these individuals were "just children," many of them were exceedingly dangerous. In fact, in many cases, juveniles are more dangerous than adults. They haven't developed impulse control, nor do they typically face longer sentences that would deter them from being violent. A good night for me, my coworker, and the sixteen teenage boys we were in charge of meant someone threw the dayroom trashcan across the room or broke a television, but no noses were broken or eyes blackened by the inmates.

None of this was new to me after a year and a half working here. The chaos had become routine. So, I mostly watched the minutes tick by, as every minute without a crisis was one minute closer to the end of my shift. I meticulously conducted and documented unit checks, making sure that all the inmates were safe and secure. I looked forward to getting everyone to bed so I could flip through a few pages of my textbook between unit checks.

The clock ticked past 7:30 p.m., and so far, so good. There wasn't much left until the unit locked down in their cells for the evening. Everyone ate dinner and finished their workouts at the gym. Most of the guys were lounging around the dayroom watching television, sprawled on the so-heavy-they-can't-be-overturned couches, or sitting at the bolted-to-the-floor spider tables. A couple of inmates worked on a jigsaw puzzle beside my desk.

My coworker and I did our best to keep our inmates—our "kids," as I affectionately called them—occupied with activities throughout the evening. Juvenile criminals with idle time tend to find increasingly creative ways to engage in criminal behavior—even in jail. The residents in my unit had a tendency to tattoo, gamble, make weapons, create escape plans, assault other residents, or self-harm if they weren't watched closely. Per the usual, I was keeping track of everyone from the staff desk in the middle of the dayroom when suddenly, out of the blue, I heard one of my inmates yell out a phrase.

"I'm going to kill myself!"

Oh no, here we go, I thought to myself.

This phrase has been weaponized as a tool of manipulation to be used against staff. When inmates shout suicidal statements across the dayroom, it generally isn't because they feel genuinely unsafe, but rather, it's a way to initiate a specific set of protocols. They did this all the time, as for them it was usually a means to an end. When an inmate yells suicidal statements, you never know what to expect next. The results can range from a "peaceful" protest to the inmate gearing up for a fight with staff.

Some residents did this to retaliate against staff. For example, inmates would make suicidal statements five minutes before a shift change to force a specific staff member to stay past the end of their shift. They couldn't leave until the resident was medically cleared from being on a suicide watch, which could take more than an hour depending on how busy the medical unit was and how long it took to reach a clinician. Retaliation from inmates stemmed from staff members issuing a "write-up" for rule breaking, enforcing activity restrictions, or something as simple as not giving an inmate an extra snack from the dining cart. Many times, an entire pod of inmates will make suicidal statements in protest to being locked down in their rooms.

Some inmates made suicidal statements for other reasons. Staff members who were assigned to a suicidal inmate were often used as an indirect means of protection. Inmates who owed gambling debts, disrespected other inmates, or had sexual convictions were often at risk of being assaulted inside the facility. Having a staff member within constant arm's length provided a degree of protection for these inmates, at least for a short period of time.

Regardless of the reasons, all suicide-prevention policies were followed to the letter after the statements were made. I was all too familiar with the drill, so I pulled out the clip-board dedicated to the task and started following protocol. I assigned the only other staff member this night to be the inmate's one-on-one, which meant he had to remain within arm's reach at all times and document his behavior to assist the mental-health clinician with making a determination during their assessment.

Like most prisons, we were chronically understaffed and overworked with no shortage of forced overtime. For safety's sake, my next task was to lock down the unit, because on the weekends, there were only two staff members in my unit with sixteen teenage boys. Although this ratio doesn't compare with ratios of many large adult prisons, we didn't monitor our inmates from a control room; we worked among them. I cycled the doors, which unlocked the pod doors and the inmates' cells, and they started walking themselves to their rooms. They, too, were all too familiar with the drill.

Click, click, click, the doors locked behind them.

Except that last door never clicked.

Moments later, the inmate who threatened self-harm violently attacked me. I braced myself as he furiously struck me numerous times in the head and face. The barrage of forceful blows only lasted about twenty seconds, but those twenty seconds changed my life forever.

A LIFE TRANSFORMED

I didn't know it yet, but from that moment on, my life as I knew it was never going to be the same. That attack not only damaged my body, but it affected my mind and completely derailed my life's path. I spent years in denial. I refused to acknowledge that this attack was going to ruin my career and the plan I had for my future.

I worked my hardest to maintain the appearance of composure. "I'll be in in the morning," I told my supervisors as I casually ate my dinner directly following the assault. *Just another day in the office,* I told myself. Little did I know at the time, the aftermath of this assault was far from over.

If you've survived something traumatic, like so many of us have, this may sound familiar, and I hope my story will resonate with you. If you have not experienced trauma firsthand, it is likely that someone in your life has. Trauma can stem from experiencing violence, abuse, natural disasters, serious car accidents, unexpected deaths, serious injury, and life-threatening illnesses, to name a few. Trauma can also create invisible injuries that we carry around with us without anyone else seeing. I hope this book can shed some light on the effects of trauma, which are all too often swept under the rug—as if avoiding them will make them go away.

I have learned through my own struggles that silence doesn't solve anything, so I am writing honestly about my trauma, not to dwell on the pain, or to brag about my progress, but to offer a lifeline to anyone who is facing what seems like an insurmountable setback. Life may never return to the way it was before the trauma, but it is possible to collect the broken pieces and rebuild your life to where it is possible to survive, and even thrive, after the worst day of your life.

Of course, getting there is hardly sunshine and roses. My life wasn't pretty for a long time after the assault. Gone were the tidy to-do lists that once held me together. I found myself fractured. I lost my identity, my ability to think and plan, and my emotional control. My life plans, which I'd so carefully organized since childhood, were completely dashed. I could pretend I took the changes in stride, but in reality, I came crashing down and hit the ground hard.

You might be in the same boat. You may think that you're on your own, that nobody will hear or understand you, and that you have to go through each day with a smile plastered on your face even though you're crumbling inside. I know I certainly did, and it took me way too long to discover that I couldn't handle everything myself—and that I didn't have to.

My hope is that by telling you the brutal truth of my ordeal, maybe you will recognize yourself in my story, and maybe you won't feel alone for as long as I did. I hope some of these words will offer some support and assist in your own healing.

In these pages, I'll share some of the lessons I've learned in the three years that have passed since the assault. Some have been most unwelcome, while others have been transformational. By showing you the ups and downs—moments when it was crucial that I pushed on for all I was worth, and also the times when I needed to accept I had done enough for one day—I hope to offer some comfort.

My hope is not only to help those currently experiencing trauma or trauma survivors, but also for their caregivers to gain some understanding—whether they're friends, family members, doctors, nurses, and even colleagues. Even if I only help one person, I will have accomplished more than I ever hoped for when I was so carefully planning my life's path all those years ago.

CHAPTER ONE

||||||||||||||||||||

BEST-LAID PLANS

When I was a kid, long before *CSI* hit the television screen, I was hooked on shows like *Cold Case Files* and *Unsolved Mysteries*. They had everything—reenacted missing persons cases, interviews with conspiracy theorists, and, of course, unsolved crimes. By the time I was ten, my mom had me hooked. Most weekdays after school would find me sitting on the couch, mentally sifting through the evidence brought forth by host Bill Kurtis, while my mother looked on from her work at the kitchen table. I was especially interested in the updates to ongoing cases: when the missing woman got found or the bank robber was identified at long last. As evidence was being presented during each segment, I found myself forming my own hypothesis about who the culprit was, and I couldn't wait until the end of the episode to see if my assumptions were correct. I was captivated by the idea that one small piece of evidence could be the key to solving the crime.

OPEN-AND-SHUT CASE

I was also fascinated by the investigators, the people who could bring order to an unorganized pile of clues and find the tiny, game-changing detail buried there. I still remember one episode featuring a skull that was broken into dozens of pieces; there seemed to be no way to determine whom it had once belonged to, but the forensic analyst was undaunted. I watched, rapt, as he methodically determined where each piece of bone belonged, until he had recreated the individual's face well enough that they were able to solve the case. I knew just how that felt; I loved solving puzzles, putting every piece in its correct place until the full picture became clear.

I always wanted to investigate things, to learn as much as I could about them. My mother understood what a little sponge I was; we did logic problems together, and she kept me supplied with workbooks and flashcards long before my school days began. Ironically, once I was in school, my teachers weren't necessarily as supportive; my first-grade teacher, for example, did not approve of me teaching myself cursive before the rest of the class had learned standard penmanship. That, apparently, was supposed to be *her* job.

Well, I didn't listen to her or to anyone who tried to keep me down. In fact, I requested extra worksheets and projects to do in class. I felt special being ahead of the other students. Eventually, in the second grade, I got bumped up to third grade, which suited me fine. Today, I can see that the move made me withdraw socially, but at the time I was happy to be able to focus on myself and what I wanted to do.

And I knew exactly what I wanted to do, as I confidently announced to the audience at a beauty pageant I entered when I was twelve. During the speech portion of the competition, like most of my peers, I spoke about my age, my extracurricular activities, and my career aspiration. I may have been the only one, however, to outline a very practical, very specific plan for doing that: I was going to be a forensic analyst and work for the FBI.

I may have been only twelve, but from that moment on, I was committed to pursuing an FBI career. My parents were equally as supportive. They understood that once I put my mind to something, I would stop at nothing to achieve my goal. In academics, in athletics, and in life, I always gave my all. I saw a clear series of steps leading to my goal. Sure, completing the steps would be hard at times, but I welcomed hard work. I was certain I could do it. Case closed.

PUTTING THE PIECES TOGETHER

By my teen years, I was doing the hard work I knew I needed to do, and it was extremely satisfying. On the physical side, I was becoming an athlete—I played softball, danced, and practiced tae kwon do. Martial arts were perfect for me because I was fiercely competitive—even with myself—and in this sport I could clearly mark my progress. I looked forward to earning the next belt color at each level and accumulating points for my performance at tournaments. One year, I won top points in my age group for forms and fighting across all of New England. I was a double crown champion, and proud of it.

I thrived on the competition. My favorite competitions were the ones that required winning multiple matches to place. I never wanted the easy win. Even more exciting were the few competitions that offered "team sparring." Team sparring involved five individuals who represented five age brackets, and the belt color didn't matter; the goal was to score as many points as possible in a ninety-second-long bout. As an orange and yellow belt, I fought for my team against black belts at the top of the age bracket. These bouts were by far the most challenging, but also my favorite. During one match at our home tournament a male black belt I was competing against drilled a kick square into my chest, hard. I never expected any man to take it easy on me, but if he was going to use that level of force, I was certainly going to match it. I wanted it more. I came back off that line with everything I had—all the tenacity and skill I could muster to score those points against a stronger, better opponent. At the end of the match, I fell short by a few points. But I made my point. Although I was a young, novice, female fighter, I wasn't going to make his win an easy one. I may have weighed a hundred pounds soaking wet, but in my mind, I was seven feet tall and weighed three hundred pounds. I believed I could take on anyone and do anything.

High school came with new challenges, but I was ready. If I wanted to get into a good college, and maybe get a much-needed scholarship, I knew I needed to get good grades and take hard classes, so I committed myself to my studies. I was never pressured by my parents to excel in school; I just looked around at my friends, who were taking the most challenging classes possible, and decided to join them. We were all competitive with one another, which pushed me to try even harder.

By this time, I was learning gymnastics and on cheerleading teams, too, though I was hardly a natural at cheering. If you had asked anyone in middle school if I'd ever be a cheerleader, they would have laughed at you, but I had developed some flexibility from my martial arts training and I was ready for a new challenge, so I went all in. After school I'd travel thirty minutes to spend two hours at tumbling practice, and I wouldn't start my homework until eight or nine at night. The next day I'd do it all again.

The physical challenge was fine with me, but I had a harder time socially. I didn't really connect with my teammates in gymnastics or cheerleading. I actually enjoyed hanging out with the football players more, because I had always been "one of the boys." I'd been playing touch football with the guys since elementary school, and even got my teeth knocked out in fourth grade. People picked on me until I got them fixed years later, but they regretted it; I threatened anyone who made fun of me. This put a huge chip on my shoulder, which impacted the way I interacted with others. By my senior year, though, I had relaxed a lot and was feeling more accepted among my peers. I'd started to fit in a little more, had my teeth fixed, and even stunned everyone when I started wearing dresses to school on game days.

My ambitions for the future initially included West Point, until I started the lengthy physical evaluation process. I passed the visual and auditory testing with no difficulties. However, during my physical entrance exam, it was determined that in order to be admitted to West Point, I would need reconstructive surgery on both of my ankles. They flagged me for chronic ankle instability after I had rolled them each three times during gymnastics and cheering. In any team photo, you can find me by looking for the ankle braces.

For the first time, I was truly stuck. Surgery wasn't an option for me financially, but if I didn't go to West Point, what would I do? I had to go back to the drawing board and come up with another plan. I wanted to continue athletics in college, but schools with good dance departments or cheering teams tend to be huge, and I wouldn't thrive in a lecture-hall environment with five hundred other students. On the other hand, many other schools seemed ordinary to me, and I was nothing if not ambitious; I wanted to go to a "good" school. I had worked hard and felt I earned it.

So, of course, I made a list. With the help of a consultant, I honed in on ten schools in the Northeast and applied to my top-three picks, which all had competitive cheering programs. Instead of getting acceptance letters in the mail, though, I was waitlisted at two and was turned down from the third. Coming from a middle-class family, I couldn't afford to be waitlisted, so back to the list I went.

None of them appealed on paper, but when we visited St. Lawrence University in upstate New York, I got a homey feeling walking around campus. Yes, it was cold, and out of the way, but it felt right. It didn't have a criminal justice program, but I knew from my research that the FBI and the other "three-letter agencies" didn't care about that because they could handle the criminal justice training themselves. Besides, most agency workers would not be carrying a gun. The agencies wanted people who could do things like analyze financial crimes, people who understood how to apply numbers to an investigation. Focusing on other areas of academia would allow me to become more well-rounded, and more desirable to future employers—or so I hoped. I decided to commit myself to this beautiful candle in the wilderness, knowing I would call this place my home. I finished my senior year in high school taking as many AP classes as I could and graduated thirteenth in my class.

Meanwhile, I was developing a clearer picture of the path ahead. My summers off between semesters were used to further enhance my credentials for future employers. I completed law enforcement internships at the local, state, and federal levels, determined to gain as much experience as I possibly could. Nothing I saw, heard, or studied scared me while interning. In fact, when I was shadowing a state trooper who was called to respond to a domestic violence call, I was ready and raring to go. Much to my despair, he dropped me off at the barracks on his way to the call for my safety. I couldn't believe he left me behind.

During the spring semester of my senior year in college, I was chosen for an internship with the U.S. Marshals in Washington, DC. It was called an internship, but it was set up like a study abroad program. Instead of going overseas, however, I lived in DC, and although I took a few classes at night, the main purpose was to gain on-the-job experience in the field that interested us most. The other students in my program shared the same drive and determination I did; we each wanted to find ourselves one day in careers such as this. Many days consisted of busywork in the IT department, but the internship program consistently offered us opportunities to learn about the different aspects of our agency, and to hear from individuals who worked with other federal agencies in the city.

We learned about the vast divisions and responsibilities of the U.S. Marshals through internal tours and presentations. We received lectures from DEA agents at the DEA Museum, toured the U.S. Capitol, visited the Library of Congress, the Naval Yard, and the National Center for Missing & Exploited Children. We attended presentations where we passed around battering rams and other equipment used in tactical operations. These trainings complimented some previous training I did during my internships—one with K-9s and another with SWAT—so they were right up my alley.

I was so thrilled by it all, I would have signed up as an agent for the Marshals' fugitive task force on the spot if I could have.

Give me the FBI's most-wanted list and let me develop an algorithm, I thought. *I'll track them down and bring them in!*

There were a lot of steps to take before that, though, and I was on it. As an undergraduate, I had already started taking graduate courses and applying for jobs. I started applying the moment I arrived for my internship in DC my senior year, and I turned in dozens of applications with the intention of returning there to work after college. I applied for a wide variety of financial jobs, from analyst jobs to book-keeping. I wanted to work for a federal agency so bad, and what better place than Washington, DC?

Even though I landed some interviews, I didn't get any offers. Breaking into the federal system takes a long time, regardless of how amazing a resume looks. And since the competition was high, even if I got an interview, it could take up to a year before starting a job. Slightly defeated, I accepted my inevitable return home to continue my job search from there.

As my work internship in Washington, DC, came to an end, a lieutenant I interned for during the previous summer called. "We have an opening in our academy," he said. "I think you should apply if you're interested. You'd be a great fit for us."

I was thrilled—and a little relieved, to be honest. During that internship, I shadowed with several officers doing ride-alongs, and I helped them work cases. I also worked on a project independently to create a new annual report, which was well received. Not only did I like the area; I grew close to those who I interned for. They knew me, and I knew them. The lieutenant was like a second dad to me. Federal agencies wanted applicants with relevant work experience, so I jumped at the opportunity and applied.

I flew home for my interview with the department, took my physical aptitude tests, and before I even graduated college, I was accepted to the police academy.

CHAPTER TWO

〃〃〃〃〃〃〃〃〃〃〃〃

COURSE CORRECTIONS

Entering the police academy was like entering an entirely new world. Although I "knew" what I was getting myself into, I can't say I was entirely prepared for it.

Academically, I was thrilled with the police academy. In the early weeks of the academy, our training consisted mostly of lectures and PowerPoint presentations on various subjects. After each lecture we were tested on the materials, which I studied hard for and passed consistently. We could have as many as five different lectures in a single day, all of which we tested on. The tests were not easy, and not all cadets passed them on the first go.

As the weeks progressed, we engaged in more hands-on learning. During the first eleven weeks of training, I learned about the laws and the practical aspects of enforcing them, from self-defense techniques to how to administer a field sobriety test. We were taught to reconstruct accident scenes and conducted active-shooter drills with paintball guns. I learned how to shoot on the gun range and how to drive tactically; I qualified the first time on every test.

I was proud of my academic achievements and successful qualifications. By the halfway point in the academy, I was ranked eleventh in my class by grade out of forty-two cadets. Considering many of these individuals had already learned this material in a part-time academy or were already working as police officers, I was proud to be competitive among others whom I respected.

I also took great pride in my abilities on the gun range. Considering I had only been taught to fire a weapon the previous year, I was a natural. I was steady in my technique and my results. I consistently hit my target and was one of a handful in my group to qualify with my weapon on the first round. When it came to knowledge, technique, and development, I was in my element.

Physically, however, I was unprepared. Although I was a competitive athlete in high school, I'd been at college for four years with a focus on my studies, not athletics. And now I worked with people who had been part-time officers or worked out every day. I'm capable of performing at a high level, but I didn't have time to train before I started.

I was discouraged to find myself one of the last people to finish most runs.

The cultural shift from college to the police academy was the hardest part. After years of striving for and receiving approval for my efforts, I had just entered a berating, military-style environment where yelling and breaking people down were the norm. Although I interned in various law enforcement departments, I was never privy to the harsh reprimands and environment. Although this was drastically different from anything I had previously experienced, it was only going to make me stronger; but that didn't mean it was going to be easy.

I also struggled with the tiny details, like making my bed exactly the way the academy expected you to. I could ace qualifying tests like driving and shooting, but when it came to uniform or bed inspections, my attempts were never quite good enough. No matter how hard I tried, there was always something wrong with my uniform. That was a struggle for me because I always aimed for perfection. In an environment where everything you did reflected your aptitude to become a police officer and reflected on the department that hired you, I didn't want to give them any reason to doubt my abilities. In this environment, *everything* was deemed important, because if you couldn't do the little things right, you couldn't be trusted to do the big things right.

BEING POLICED

Everything from physical activity to emotional expression was tightly controlled; rules—written and unwritten—governed my every move, even when I thought nobody was looking.

In my eleventh week at the academy, just a few weeks before graduation, we had a class about suicide. On the first day, a courageous young man and woman came to talk about their personal suicide attempts to help us learn ways to prevent these tragedies from happening. They shared their feelings with us, how they'd felt like burdens to their families, and how they'd felt as if they just didn't belong. It was heartbreaking. They described their suicide plans and walked us through every move they made on what they planned to be their "last" day. They also told us what made them decide not to go through with it. Their stories were so powerful that when I got back to my room that night and reflected on them, I was moved to tears.

After decompressing, I left those feelings of empathy in my room. I knew there was a time and place for everything. The next morning, I walked into the lecture hall ready to tackle the challenges that were awaiting me. The topic of that day's class was processing suicide crime scenes. We were presented with graphic and grisly photographs, and the instructor described what happened in their final moments based on evidence presented in the pictures. Unlike the day before, there was no empathy on my part. The "human" aspect was gone, and I focused on the knowledge that was to be gained and the details that could potentially differentiate a homicide from a suicide. Back to business.

My new roommate, meanwhile, had apparently been concentrating on me and the tears I had shed in the privacy of my own room the night before. She broke the "no tattling" code of police culture by sharing the story of my private emotional display far and wide. My moment of empathy quickly made it to the academy cadre, and I was called into the office. When I walked in, I was shocked to see members from the top of my department sitting there waiting for me. "This is the eleventh week. We shouldn't be having issues this far in," one of them barked at me.

"Is it true you cried after listening to the suicide presentations?" my captain asked.

"Yes," I replied, knowing all too well where this conversation was going. "I had a lot of empathy for them." I expected at least a nod of acknowledgment in return, but he went on to his next question.

"You also cried when you got pepper sprayed, didn't you?"

Yes, I cried the first time I got pepper sprayed. It hurt. I swore out of pain and therefore "didn't maintain my professionalism." Another cadet—who was recruited by a more prestigious agency—broke down into a complete panic attack and needed consoling by the cadre, but apparently my swearing out of pain and frustration was unacceptable by my department's standards.

I was getting anxious about the questioning, so I simply nodded, hoping this would all end soon. But there was more.

"And you cried when you got tased, correct?"

He was referring to the taser training that I signed up for voluntarily at the department prior to entering the academy. For the record, I didn't weep or anything. Yes, I wiped away a couple of tears in the bathroom after being shot with the taser, but frankly, it was an automatic response from my body due to the shock. I didn't have to undergo that training. One of the instructors, a former marine, even refused to participate when he was hired. I remember him saying, "if Parris Island didn't make me a man, then nothing will." I specifically opted in to that training to show those who hired me that I was willing to put myself in a position that was uncomfortable and that I wasn't afraid of a little pain. Unfortunately, that was now being used against me.

I tried again to explain myself, emphasizing that I had completed every task asked of me and had even maintained my composure when looking at horrifying suicide-scene photos. I didn't cry because I couldn't handle it; I cried out of compassion for those people who felt as if they didn't belong anywhere in the world—in the privacy of my own room at the end of the day. I thought I had proven how tough I was.

It clearly wasn't enough. As soon as the questioning ended, they presented me with resignation and termination papers and told me to choose one. They had made their decision before I had even entered the room: I was too sensitive for the job. I don't have what it takes. I would not be graduating with my class.

I was in complete disbelief. I signed the resignations papers without saying another word—and I certainly wasn't going to cry, even though I wanted to.

I was immediately escorted past my peers to my room to pack my things. It was absolutely humiliating. Everyone stood outside their rooms wondering what was going on, but they knew better than to ask. They just stood there and looked on. Silent and grim, I folded my clothes, squeezed everything into my duffel bag, and walked out of the police academy.

I might have not said a word out loud, but in my head, I was reeling. I'd done eight years of work and planning only to end up with a black mark on my record that would never go away. And now I had to go home and tell my parents that I was forced to resign from the position I'd worked so hard to get, the job that was supposed to be the first step toward my career goal.

I still couldn't wrap my head around the fact that I was penalized for displaying empathy in private. We had undergone so many trainings about how cops are at higher risk of domestic violence, alcoholism, suicide, etc. because they couldn't cope with various aspects of the job. My coping skill was to cry and process what I needed to, in a time and place that was appropriate.

I felt my future was over. My training was over, my job was over, and my career was over before it even got started. Maybe they were right. Maybe I didn't have what it takes to be in this line of work. Maybe I was too sensitive. Maybe everything was for nothing.

For the first time in my life, I had no idea what to do next. Should I give it another try, or go in an entirely different direction? I didn't know, and I didn't want to talk to anyone about it, because I was so embarrassed. My parents encouraged me to pursue other avenues; the idea of being in constant danger didn't sit well with my mother. At the time, police officers were also becoming targets of hate crimes. There were several stories of cops being ambushed and shot at randomly, simply for wearing a badge, so I understood where she was coming from.

But I didn't have experience doing anything else. This was my entire life.

During an unexpected visit, my aunt stopped by to offer some encouragement after hearing the news. I was initially chagrined by her visit; I didn't want anyone to know about my failures. She had come to ask me about what my plans were and what was next for me. I repeated some of the things I had discussed with my parents, like seeking a career in the financial sector, but nothing I was overly excited about. She kept prodding me until I admitted that criminal justice was still my passion and I couldn't just give up on it. She seemed like she already knew that, though— she just helped me get around to admitting it.

My journey wasn't over; it was time for a new plan.

I was determined to address all of the shortcomings that the police academy pointed out. Now that I was back home, I started back up at my local CrossFit gym. I had built a strong foundation at the academy, but I was ready to push myself to the next level. Physical endurance: check. My department also questioned my pain tolerance after showing tears while being tased and pepper sprayed. Message received, toughen up. To address this shortcoming, I got my first tattoo, a twelve-hour rib piece. I decided on a meaningful piece, a koi fish with two lotus flowers. Koi fish are known for their tenacity and their ability to climb rushing streams and waterfalls, and they represent perseverance and overcoming adversity. The koi is accompanied by two lotus flowers, which cannot bloom without mud. I was determined to sit through this piece without a single tear, and I was successful. I was ready to give my dream a second chance. I polished up my interview speech:

"I'm proficient in marksmanship, self-defense, field testing, and all of the other skills you can see from my academy records. I was unprepared during my first attempt at the academy, but I've learned from my mistakes. I'm better, faster, and stronger now and ready to give you 100 percent."

While I started over by taking new fitness tests at a different academy, I met some officers who were recruiting for the state prison. Never in my life had I considered working in a prison, but they were touting the excellent pay and promise of a raise after a couple of months, so I was intrigued. I started looking at different correctional opportunities, applied, and got offered two positions, one at an adult prison and one at a juvenile prison. After some careful thought, I accepted the job at the juvenile prison. It felt like a fresh start.

The job appealed to me on a practical level—it was a short commute from home and it came with good benefits. I was also interested in guiding and mentoring troubled youth. I had tutored kids academically and felt like I could help these kids change their path in life. Since they were young, they had a chance at a better outcome. Maybe I could be part of that.

Fresh out of school with student debt staring me in the face, the money sounded good to me, too. Also, the chance to prove I could hold my own working in a corrections facility was important to me. If I excelled at the job, I'd gain a little street cred, something my bruised ego sorely needed after the fiasco at the police academy.

I didn't realize how naïve I was until several weeks on the job. They broke us in slowly, beginning with classes in the west wing of the building, where the comfortable offices and conference rooms were. We spent eight weeks taking classes there, including ethics, crisis intervention, CPR, self-defense, active listening, and correctional fatigue (burnout) prevention. Some classes were hands-on, and some involved guest speakers, but we spent a lot of time looking at PowerPoint presentations. The lecture format wasn't a problem for me; I've loved learning. Even though I had heard much of this in the police academy, I was happy to absorb whatever information they could give me.

I only got a real sense of what the work entailed at lunchtime, when the instructors encouraged us to spend some time in the cafeteria with the inmates and staff. Just navigating the hallways on the way to the cafeteria was fraught—these kids knew what was up and harassed us verbally, shouting things like, "Oh, fresh meat!" It wasn't unexpected, because we wore different clothes and definitely stood out, so we just tried to keep a straight face and take it in stride.

We were encouraged to connect with the inmates during lunch and to build rapport, because we needed the kids to listen to us when the time came. If they didn't respect or trust us, there was no hope of that. Fortunately for me, we had lunch with the girls' unit, so I could make relatable small talk with the girls, while still maintaining some image of authority. It was a delicate balance. I wanted to appear in control, but in reality, I was only a couple of years older than some of these girls. In my mind, these girls reminded me of people I'd known in high school.

On the surface there appeared to be little difference between this cafeteria and a high school lunchroom. There were teenage girls of different ages, looks, and backgrounds, just like in high school. If you were there, you'd have heard the same kinds of conversations, too, discussing which girls were best friends yesterday but not today, gossiping about who said what about who. You'd watch the boys vying for power in a social hierarchy familiar to anyone who ever attended a public high school. If one of the more powerful kids was getting money on his canteen account from his parents, for instance, the other kids would jockey for a chance to be his foot soldier, as they could be easily bribed with canteen items, like snacks and soda. Unfortunately, anyone who received money who was lower on the hierarchy was at risk of being threatened and extorted for those few extra snacks.

Everyone had their parts to play.

ON-THE-JOB TRAINING

Our little class of seven new staff members, however, didn't know our parts yet—even though our instructors tried to show us what it would be like on the floor.

Our superiors warned us that the inmates would be disruptive but assured us there were procedures in place for dealing with whatever came up. If there was a fight in the dining room, for example, the first staff member there would "call a code" to alert other staff and bring them running. One staff member would get the uninvolved residents out of the room and escort them back to their unit, while the rest of us would try to get the fighters under control.

Once we had enough staff members present, we could deploy a restraint technique we'd been trained in extensively. In this technique, staff members work in pairs to hold the inmate's arms against their body so they can't push outward. This takes the wind out of their sails without any pain and is often used to separate fighters or to walk unruly inmates to the Special Management Unit (SMU). Jail policy dictated that a certain number of staff members had to be present for each combatant before the technique could be used, otherwise staff were in danger of getting caught in the crosshairs. So, if two inmates were fighting, we couldn't deploy the restraint technique until enough officers were present. The boys knew this policy, though, so they'd usually stop fighting right as enough staff arrived to break up the fight.

Once the kids were under control, they either went to medical (if they were injured) or to the SMU for a supervised timeout. While most of the units in the building had three levels with three pods and a dayroom, the SMU was a singular room with cells around the perimeter and an observation room in the middle. The observation room was reserved for the most extreme situations. The SMU was designed for the officer in the unit to have eyes on all inmates from the staff desk.

Following a fight and medical evaluation, fighters were usually held on opposite sides of the SMU for a forty-five-minute timeout. Depending on the inmate's behavior prior to the fight, unit staff could determine whether to release the inmate back to his unit, or to keep him in the SMU for an extended period of time, which could mean days.

Meanwhile, the violation would be thoroughly documented.

A fight gets written up as a major violation. The victim could press charges against their assailant, but that rarely happened. Major violations like fights brought on consequences, usually activity restrictions, like being confined to the pod for a certain number of hours with no gym or outside time. Minor violations, on the other hand, were mostly nonviolent incidents that had more to do with disrespecting the rules or officers. While major violations included fights, tattooing, and building weapons, minor violations included swearing, not keeping their rooms tidy, and disobeying an officer's orders. Both violations warranted a write-up, but there was no appeal process for minor violations.

If the kids didn't sign their write-ups for major violations, the write-ups would go before a board that was supposed to review the incident and decide if the inmate was guilty of the violation. Most of the time, however, these write-ups never made it back, which meant that the consequences would not be approved. The kids knew this (of course) and would purposely refuse to sign to avoid suffering any consequences (unless they picked up additional charges).

For minor violations, the maximum consequence was a two-day activity restriction, but because there was no way for the inmate to appeal it, they had to serve it. For staffers, this was our only outlet to serve punishments to keep the inmates accountable.

The procedures and policies in place made it seem manageable, but nothing was as easy as it looked. Dealing with these inmates day in and day out was less about following the rules and more about being a clever, on-the-spot negotiator.

During our training, our instructors told us stories, like the time a few kids in one unit camped out in the drop ceiling and refused to come down. Warnings were given, punishments threatened, and still they wouldn't come out. Finally, someone on staff stopped yelling at them and instead asked them a question: "What will it take for you to come out?" they shouted up toward the ceiling.

"Skittles and soda," came the quick reply. Staff retrieved some Skittles and soda and—just like that—down they came.

The inmates knew how the system worked. They knew the staff's powers were limited, and they knew how to manipulate those limits to get what they wanted. In this particular incident, there was no pepper spray or tactical team. Those were not options for staff. Instead, there was bargaining. Skittles and soda. That's all it took.

Despite our training and hearing many stories of previous incidents, we still didn't understand what a day on the job would *actually* look like. Our reality check was coming, though.

WHAT SHIFTS WERE *ACTUALLY* LIKE

After we completed our training, we shadowed different units and worked different shifts, doing the least glamorous, most physically demanding parts of the job, like unit checks. Unit checks meant physically checking every single room, multiple times an hour for the entire shift, making sure that the doors were locked, that everyone was following the rules, and that nobody was self-harming or being harmed. There were three predominant shifts: the morning shift from 6:30 a.m. to 3 p.m., which we called first shift; the afternoon shift from 2 p.m. to 10:30 p.m., which we called second shift; and then the overnight shift from 10:15 p.m. to 6:45 a.m., also known as the third shift.

The unit checks during training were pretty good practice for the shift I started on, which were overnights on the moderate-risk girls' unit. I went in when everyone was already sleeping (or at least they were supposed to be), so my first responsibility was to inventory tools like mops, brooms, nail clippers, and razors to make sure everything was accounted for (if something was missing, it could mean they were being fashioned into a weapon, which would warrant a protocol). Next, I reviewed the logbook to see if anything significant happened during the prior shift I should be aware of. For the rest of the night after that, I'd walk through the unit and check the rooms more than thirty times.

You would think that the overnight shift would be immune

from much excitement, but you would be mistaken. Sometimes the inmates wouldn't sleep, so they'd often cause a ruckus and irritate other inmates who were trying to sleep. Sometimes there would be an incident that hadn't been resolved during the day, so the incident would still be unfolding as we came in. If second shift couldn't resolve incidents, they were passed onto staff working the overnight shift—which meant significantly fewer people to handle them.

This happened more often than you'd think. On one particular day, for example, the girls in one of the units took their mattresses and placed them in their doorway so that their cell doors couldn't close. Those on second shift didn't want to deal with it, so they just let the girls lie on their mattresses with their doors open. They didn't want to cause a code, because then that meant they would have to finish writing their reports before leaving for the day. Instead, they decided to let third shift deal with it—the shift with fewer people, no less! The inmates were supposed to be locked in their cells by the time my shift started, but there were plenty of days when the minute I walked into work at 10:15 p.m., I was immediately thrust into dealing with one thing or another.

A year or so before I started, the jail saw one of its most egregious incidents, which happened during the overnight shift. Three inmates in the high-risk unit thought it would be a good idea to try to escape the facility. From their pod, they had to break through two continuous doors to get outside. They brutally beat a male staff member (who was close to retirement) while successfully breaking through the first door. Fortunately, they were unable to do the same for the second door and were thus apprehended. Since they were all over the age of eighteen, they were sent to adult jail. This incident led the juvenile facility to change some of its policies, including measures to increase staff safety if doors needed to be opened at night.

Thankfully, I never endured anything that severe during overnights, but they were terrible, nonetheless. You never get used to being awake at night. It's an unnatural and dysregulating schedule. When was I supposed to eat? To sleep? Everything was upside down, and it was hard for me to find a solid rhythm. So, after six months, I accepted a position in the high-risk male unit on the weekend shift. My new schedule had me working second shift on Fridays and Saturdays (2 p.m. to 10:30 p.m.) and first shift on Sundays, Mondays, and Tuesdays (6:30 a.m. to 3 p.m.).

Many of my coworkers considered this unit the worst because the inmates were the most difficult to deal with. They were the most aggressive, impulsive, and had the most mental-health issues. But I wasn't deterred. I wanted to be in that unit specifically because of the unit manager and how he ran the unit. The rules for inmates in the high-risk unit were much more structured and clear—do A, B, and C; don't do X, Y, and Z. If an inmate broke the rules, they were held more accountable and suffered the consequences. The two moderate-risk units in the facility were much more lax with their rules and consequences, which didn't appeal to me. How can you expect to change their criminal behaviors if they aren't even being held accountable in prison?

The inmates in the high-risk unit knew the rules inside and out—but that didn't mean they always followed them—they were still adolescent kids, after all. If the unit ran smoothly from dusk to dawn, it usually happened during the week, mostly because there were more people for inmates to engage with. In addition to the officers and administrators, there were teachers, clinicians, therapists, various school faculty, medical personnel, mentors, volunteers, and so on.

As a juvenile facility, inmates went to school Monday through Friday, from 8 a.m. to 3 p.m. Our facility had an accredited high school and even offered some college courses. In order for each inmate to be released, they needed to complete a set of requirements, what we called "their program" (in other words, their sentencing). A program was tailored specifically to each inmate. Unlike in a public high school setting where all the fourteen-year-olds are in ninth grade and all the fifteen-year-olds are in tenth grade, our classrooms were mixed (but not coed). Each inmate had their own education plan, and the teachers tailored the work assignments to each individual's needs.

I was surprised to learn that several inmates in their teens didn't know how to read or write. There was one sixteen-year-old kid who really struggled with reading and writing. Having experienced an abusive childhood, he was certainly rough around the edges. One day, he hated me. The next day, I was his saving grace. I often escorted him to his reading class with a teacher who was in her seventies or eighties. She was just the sweetest woman, perfect for working with our problematic teens. She was so endearing to him, and he loved her for it. She worked with him using a computer reading program. At the end of each chapter, he'd get a certificate, congratulating him on his progress.

This might not seem like a big deal, but for a kid who grew up in an environment that didn't value education and learning, it was huge. After each certificate, he'd boast about himself, showing off his certificate to me. Those certificates made him so proud, and even though these moments came few and far between, it was a treat to see the positive effects of our programs.

Attending class was a requirement for all inmates, unless they already graduated from high school (our jail housed "juveniles" up to age twenty-one). Line staff were responsible for escorting inmates to and from class, but our presence wasn't required in the actual classroom. During their time in class, we returned to the units to conduct unit checks and room inspections. After school, we would escort them back to their respective units, but there were still a variety of options for the inmates to do in terms of activities. In addition to the amount of time on their sentence and their educational requirements, their program also included a variety of therapy programs. The jail had incredible therapy programs, designed specifically to suit each inmate's needs, whether that was substance abuse, violent tendencies, counseling for sexual offenders, and so on. Depending on their program, each inmate met with their clinician or therapist once or twice a week. They also participated in group therapy sessions with other inmates.

With how the days were structured during the week, our jobs as line staff were considerably less hectic because the schedule offered opportunities for the inmates to engage with other adults. Sometimes that meant an inmate spent more time in the library, assisting the librarian with a project. Inmates often requested to see their therapist, which we would grant if the therapist was available. Some would work in laundry or in dining. And for those who proved to be trustworthy, they would work off-grounds to gain on-the-job experience while serving their time.

Inmates were better behaved midweek by virtue of having a concrete schedule and the option to interact with different adults. They also knew the "big guns" were in the building—administrators who had more influence on their progress in completing their program (meaning they had the power to hand out consequences). Over the weekends, however, it was just us and the inmates. While there were upwards of fifty staff, faculty, medical personnel, etc. on the premises during the week, staff would shrink to ten to fifteen over the weekends—and our facility housed anywhere between eighty and one hundred inmates.

Needless to say, weekends turned into the wild, wild West.

The kids did crazy stuff. and it was never, ever smooth sailing—like the girls who ate random mushrooms growing in the yard so they could be sent to the local hospital (and thereby leave the facility), or the kid who climbed into the drop ceiling of the SMU. He kicked out the tiles, set off the sprinklers, and made the light fixtures spark. The other kids in the unit thought they were going to get electrocuted. That night was one for the books.

They made booze. They started fires. On a good night, kids pulled fire alarms, DVD players got smashed, fights broke out in the hallways, and ten-gallon Gatorade tubs went flying. On a bad night, we ended up running a wet vac in the pods because some kid popped the sprinkler in his room and flooded the place; or we'd have four kids on retaliatory suicide watches at the same time. On a terrible night, an inmate would assault staff, causing serious injury, or a suicide attempt would come close to being successful. Terrible nights, unfortunately, were all too common.

Every weekend, there was a fight or a suicide threat, often stemming from entanglements between the girls' units and the boys' units. It usually started with the girls—maybe one inmate had gotten bad news from home and another inmate didn't like her getting all the attention, so she barricaded herself in her room and threatened self-harm. When the code call went out over the radio, the boys heard it, and they reacted. Maybe one of them had been exchanging letters with this girl, and then he would get agitated and start a fight in the boys' unit.

Each incident like this often required us to send the disruptive inmate to the medical department, but he would refuse to go. In that case, officers would physically escort the inmate to medical, which would make us even more shorthanded on the unit. Of course, once we assembled enough staff to physically escort the inmate, he'd usually laugh and say, "Just kidding, guys. I'll walk."

The inmates were experts at "playing the game." They knew our hands were tied as far as what the administration would allow us to do, so they knew how to work the system to their advantage. For instance, if an inmate defied us by refusing to join the rest of the group for dinner, he knew we still had to bring him his food. We tried to fight it, but if I said no—as I often did—he would keep fighting me, yelling, and throwing things until I called a code that brought staff from other units to help. The kids also understood the jail's hierarchy. They paid attention to who outranked whom, so they'd often act out to get a supervisor from one of the "less strict" units on the scene who would overrule me—and it usually worked, which only reinforced their behavior. Next thing I knew, the supervisor would grant the troublemaker's request, and he would be sitting smugly in the dayroom eating his meal and watching TV. It was infuriating.

Sometimes, we couldn't piece incidents together, because the inmates were dishonest (I know, shocking). During one of my second shifts, the kids were getting ready for bed as I stood at the staff desk. The coworker on shift with me was conducting unit checks, but somehow didn't notice that one of the doors to an inmate's room was unlocked (they're supposed to be locked at all times). Ten minutes later, an inmate (convicted of attempted murder and who frequently fantasized about being a serial killer) approached me and said, "Hey, Plante! Look at my face!" His face was full-blown red—not the holding-your-breath-type red, but more like a severe-case-of-rosacea-type red. The blood vessels in his face and eyes popped, and he looked like a character out of a bad Halloween flick. Having been through countless hours of training (and thanks to watching all those CSI episodes), I immediately knew what had happened: attempted strangulation. I've seen this before. In domestic violence cases, if a woman is strangled, it can cause blood vessels in the eyes to burst. It was one thing to see pictures of it in course books, but having someone staring at me with his face blown up like a volcano after someone injected red ink in their eyeballs was a sight to see. This kid was already scary-looking on his own, and this new look certainly wasn't doing him any favors.

What I couldn't immediately tell was whether it was by his own doing or someone else's.

I told him to sit down and chill while I called medical and additional staff to assist. "What happened?" I asked him. He said another inmate left his door open on purpose so that he could kill himself in his room. Apparently, it was planned out. When the other inmate left to shower, he agreed to leave his door open. Well, that certainly happened, but when we interviewed the other inmate, he denied everything. In fact, he was the one who walked in on him suffocating in his room, and apparently he kicked him out.

A classic he-said-she-said scenario left us with nothing but a written report, a suicide watch, and a crazy story to tell. The truth, to this day, is still unknown.

Incidents in the facility weren't all bad and malicious. Although these inmates were criminals, they were young, immature, adolescent kids. They were naturally mischievous and loved to play pranks. They would often try sneaking into another person's room and hiding under the bed, for example, just to see if they could get away with it (and they did on a few occasions). They just wanted their own version of a sleepover.

Despite their criminal ways, our inmates were teenagers with unfortunate upbringings, a limited view of the world, and raging hormones—a lovely combination. Naturally, as you might expect, there were a lot of romance quarrels, but not in the way you might think. Life in jail isn't structured for relationships since males and females are kept separated. The only time they were in the same room was during chapel, and even then, the girls were on one side and the boys on the other. They weren't allowed to mingle or engage with one another before, during, or after chapel, either. Once a week, line staff escorted them to chapel and then escorted them back to their units afterward.

Despite basically no opportunities to be together, our inmates still had relationships—and they took them *very seriously*. Since they couldn't see one another, inmates resorted to letter writing. They'd hide notes to one another in common places like the gym, the library, or in classrooms. Almost everyone wrote letters—and these letters signified relationship status. People were together if they were writing letters to one another. If an inmate wrote a letter to more than one person, that was considered cheating. If one girl wrote a letter to another girl's "man," the girls would start world war III—throwing punches, pulling hair, and gouging eyes out.

One couple wrote letters of support to each other, which was sweet to see. They were both lower-functioning teenagers who experienced terribly abusive childhoods. I'm guessing their commonalities are what made them fall for each other. The jail intercepted all communication between inmates (for safety reasons, among others), and they were full of phrases like "We can do this," and, "You're doing so good. Keep it up." They were encouraging one another to make wise decisions so that they could successfully complete their programs, be released, and be together in the outside world. Again, although very few and far between, these were the moments that gave me hope that maybe some of these individuals could have a better future.

While most people my age looked forward to weekends, I looked forward to them ending. Going to work on Monday filled me with great ease since the kids had more rigid schedules and it wasn't just us stuck in a unit with them all day.

Even so, things were still eventful. After escorting them to their classes, we conducted room searches. The things we found in those rooms amazed me. The most common contraband were metal paper clips, sandpaper, pencils, and pens. The paper clips were sanded down to a sharp point with sandpaper stolen from carpentry class. The inmates stashed pencils to break the graphite apart and crush it into powder. With these tools and a bit of hair conditioner, the residents created homemade, and not very sanitary, tattoo pens.

Many of the boys had prison tattoos, from crosses to girls' names, scrawled all over their bodies, even on their faces. Tattooing was considered a major violation. Once staff noticed a new tattoo (usually the next day), the inmate got written up and suffered some minor consequences. Despite the unsanitary method, tattoos were usually harmless since they didn't involve anyone but themselves. Problems arose, however, when inmates passed their homemade tattoo needles to other inmates.

I was notorious for noticing new tattoos on my inmates—even if they already had full sleeves. I was also notorious for writing them up. There were many Friday nights when I would first walk into the unit after my two days off, and one of my inmates would come up to me at the staff desk the moment I walked in and say: "Plante, check out my new tattoos!"

"Your arm is going to fall off if you don't stop that," I would say, shaking my head. We would then discuss consequences.

He knew I was going to notice them anyway, so he tried to get the write-up out of the way while I was in a good mood, fresh off my days off. Some inmates tattooed entire sleeves without any serious issues. Others, however, weren't so lucky.

One night, one of the boys showed me his arm after tattooing himself. The skin surrounding the fresh tattoo was bright red and puffy—clearly infected. Using a Sharpie, I drew a circle around the affected area and noted the time before calling medical. The medical unit was also policy driven, so it was reluctant to see residents without a "sick call slip," which would result in them being seen in the next few days. Thankfully, I had a good rapport with most of the nursing staff, and they respected me enough to know that when I was adamant about something, it was serious.

"Listen," I told the nurses. "This is serious. He has a serious infection going on. Can I bring him over now?"

Thankfully they listened. By the time the nurse saw him that evening, the redness and swelling had spread half-an-inch outside the circle, and his veins were turning a different color. Medical staff injected him with antibiotics and transferred him to a hospital because of the severity of his infection.

On another night, I got a tip that one kid made a shank

and hid it in the holes at the bottom of the steel door in his room. It might sound crazy, but this wasn't the first time inmates tried to hide things inside their doors. Residents often used the lip of the door to hide prohibited items, but then they would fall into the crevice, making it harder to retrieve. It was one of many "not so secret" hiding spots. This spot seemed too small to hide a weapon, but I went to check anyway—and there was something there. It had slid too far into the door for me to retrieve it, and I couldn't tell what it was.

To retrieve the weapon, my unit manager had to call maintenance to remove the steel door off the hinges, but we got it. A plastic toothbrush shaved down to a three-inch spike. It was both impressive and terrifying. We also found a second toothbrush that wasn't as sharp, but appeared to have fallen too far into the door for the inmate to retrieve. We had heard several rumors throughout the week that there were weapons in our unit, and that they were intended for a specific target. The inmate spent a week in the SMU as we continued to search for any additional weapons or threats. I can't even imagine what could have happened if I hadn't investigated that tip to the extent of having the door removed. Had the inmate been able to retrieve those weapons, I can only imagine what he would have done.

I lived for moments like this, though—moments I knew our vigilance had made a difference in a kid's life. Countless times on unit checks, we stopped someone from self-harming or committing suicide. Unfortunately, we were not successful every time. I may never stop grieving for the ones we couldn't save.

TWO CASES; TWO DIFFERENT ENDINGS

Although threats of suicide were often used by inmates as a manipulation strategy, there were also times when threats of suicide were very real. During my time working at the jail, I experienced two self-harming incidents with drastically different endings.

The first incident happened after only two months on the job. When I first started, I worked overnights on the girls' unit and successfully started to build rapport with some of them. One of the girls stopped taking her medication for a significant mental illness. She was a few months away from turning eighteen, with only a short time left on her sentence. Despite working the overnight shift, I noticed significant changes in her behavior. One night, between my checks, she rang the buzzer for her room. When I went to see what she needed, she showed me a cut on her wrist that was bleeding down her arm. She had cut herself with a piece of concrete from the floor. The necessary steps were taken to bring her to medical and place her on a suicide watch. It was the first time I saw blood on the night shift.

Over the next few shifts, I was on high alert. As I was still new, I made sure I knew what code to call and the steps that needed to be taken if there was a serious medical event in the middle of the night. After a few days, the suicide watch was lifted, but my concern didn't diminish.

When you check on every inmate in the unit more than thirty times in a shift for days and days on end, you start to recognize how everyone sleeps. Several days later, as I started my first round of unit checks for the night after everyone had gone to bed, this girl was lying down as if she was sleeping, but something wasn't right. Something didn't feel right to me. Since she had engaged in self-harm earlier in the week, I listened to my gut and immediately called for responders and for medical.

When that response team arrived and popped her door open, they pulled the blanket off her and found that she had opened the vein in her elbow with a small but sharp piece of concrete from the floor. She had lost a couple of pints of blood, but because the metal bed frames had a lip all the way around, it caught her blood and prevented it from hitting the floor. Even though she looked like she was sleeping, she was actually bleeding out under her covers. She was still conscious, though, so our response team quickly applied a tourniquet and transported her to the hospital.

Thankfully, we got to her in time.

Meanwhile, back at the jail, I was left doing unit checks with a room that looked like a crime scene. The blood from the bed had spilled on the floor as medical moved her out of the room. The commotion also woke some of the other residents, who could see the blood in her room, so I had to calm their nerves and concerns.

I was formally recognized for my actions, which surprised me. My supervisor wrote me a commendation and I received a plaque, as did others who had critical roles in responding to the incident. I was just happy that I was in the right place, at the right time, and I knew enough to trust my gut instinct in that moment.

The inmate spent several weeks away from the facility, but eventually returned to the jail. As soon as she returned, I started having horrific nightmares at night, even though we saved her life. She haunted my dreams. One night, I dreamt that I was on her suicide watch when she wanted to take a shower. I escorted her and remained on watch, but when she asked me to fetch some shampoo from her room, I agreed. I left her. Alone. I took two steps and froze. I knew what I had done—a stomach-churning "Oh shit!" moment— and was paralyzed by intense fear and panic. Having only taken my eyes off of her for a few seconds, I immediately turned back to the shower, only to find her limp body hanging from the showerhead.

Saving her life felt like a miracle of sorts, since I acted on just a gut feeling. But thoughts and questions plagued me afterward. What if I hadn't made the call? I saved her once, but could I do it again? Could I save the next inmate who attempted? I felt an incredible amount of pressure, as well as an overwhelming fear that I might not succeed next time.

After she returned to the facility, I spent many nights posted outside of her room on suicide watch, keeping her in constant sight. When I wasn't the one on her suicide watch, my mind was restless, and an incredible tension spread throughout my body. I felt like no one could keep her safe and that it was all up to me. During unit checks, I was terrified that I would return to her room and it would be too late.

I tried to keep things light, so I engaged in positive interactions with the inmate, doing anything to avoid reliving that night again. She had an incredible voice and often sang the song *Landslide* by the Dixie Chicks as I sat on her watch, which kept both of our minds off of the things we didn't want to think about. Internally, however, my nerves hadn't subsided, and conversing with someone who could have died gave me incredible anxiety.

She completed her time, and upon her eighteenth birthday, she was released. I gave her a hug the night she left. It was one of those hugs where there were so many things to say on both sides, but we didn't say anything. I wished nothing but the best for her, even though I knew she'd have an uphill battle with whatever she decided to do. To this day, I still think about her when I hear that song.

The second incident happened after just over a year of me working at the jail. I had switched to days by this point, but this particular day, I was working an overtime shift. I was assigned a rover role, which meant I acted like a gopher, moving between units depending on where an extra staff member was needed. Lucky for me, there was an outbreak of scabies in the facility, and when none of my macho coworkers volunteered to take on the job of disinfecting my unit, I raised my hand to do it.

I wore a lesser version of a hazmat suit that was entirely too big (which was quite the comical sight) and worked through the unit, spraying each space from top to bottom, focusing on anything with fabric—couches, beds, carpet, etc. As I finished spraying every inch of my own high-risk unit, I heard a code come over the radio from the neighboring unit. The code used meant an inmate was trying to inflict self-harm.

I dropped the sprayer and ran toward the unit.

Because I was a rover that afternoon, that also meant I was designated as a responder. And due to my physical location when the code was called—being the closest to that unit—I was the first respondent on scene.

As I entered the unit, I had to run past the staff bubble, the room where staff wrote reports and kept paperwork. A staff member in the bubble was retrieving a cutdown tool out of a lockbox—a hooked blade used as a lifesaving tool to help cut through fabric. As I ran past the staff bubble, they passed the tool to me as if we were passing a baton in a sprinted race. I ran into one of the pods, up the stairs, and down the row of rooms, heading toward the last door on the left. As I entered the room, at first I didn't see anything. The bed was empty, and there was nobody in my direct line of sight.

As I turned around, there he was, behind the door.

Oh, my, God.

I immediately used the tool to cut him down, hoping I got to him in time. When I laid him down on the floor, I put my hand under his nose and felt some air come out. *Oh, thank God! He's breathing!*

Unfortunately, I was wrong. Moving him to the floor forced any remaining oxygen out of his body, but I didn't realize that in the moment. Medical nurses arrived behind me and directed me to start CPR. I started chest compressions while the nurses prepared mouth guards to administer breathing. Everything was on autopilot for me. As I did each compression, I directed another staff member to count for me. *One... two...three...four...* As I pushed down on his chest, I kept looking at the inmate, expecting him to come back to life—like a scene from a movie.

Due to the severity of this situation, we immediately called for outside medical services. I continued the compressions for fifteen minutes while waiting for the EMTs to arrive, which seemed like forever. Once they finally arrived, they took over CPR and started injecting him with various drugs. The EMTs worked swiftly, but everything I saw seemed to be happening in slow motion. I couldn't comprehend the extent of what I was just a part of. I stood behind them as they worked, continuing to hope that I would see him regain consciousness and that he would be okay.

At this point, my building supervisor approached me. "Plante, go downstairs." I started walking backward toward the stairs but stopped just shy of where they started. In my mind, there was no way I was leaving him. Not now.

"Plante. Go downstairs. *Now*." I don't think he wanted me to see any more. He wanted to remove me from the situation, but I didn't want to leave.

Minutes felt like hours. I finally overheard them say they were able to get his heartbeat back. *We did it! We saved him! He's going to be okay!* I was so relieved. I watched as they loaded him into the ambulance and drove away to the hospital.

As the commotion settled, staff members were all left in a state of shock. It was one of the most devastating situations to happen in that building in more than a decade.

The incident happened in the afternoon while the other inmates from the unit were otherwise preoccupied at the gym, so thankfully none of them witnessed anything. My supervisor ordered me and another staff member into his office, where we sat in silence, isolated from the facility to decompress what we had just witnessed, and started writing our reports. Additional supervisors came in to check on us. Several supervisors encouraged me to go home, but I didn't want to. I had every intention of finishing the rest of my sixteen-hour shift—I was fine. After some convincing, however, I accepted their advice and went home, as the emotional exhaustion had taken its toll.

I returned to work the next day for my regularly scheduled shift and maintained that everything was business as usual, even though that was far from the truth. Administrators came in that Sunday to check on the staff and residents after such a dramatic event. The superintendent of the facility pulled me aside to check in on me. "Hey, Plante. How are you doing?"

"'I'm fine," I replied. "How's the inmate doing?"

"He's alive, but on life support. Unfortunately, he doesn't have any brain function."

"If anything happens, can you call me and let me know?" I asked. I was concerned about getting unfavorable news directly before the start of my next shift and having to conceal my grief and keep myself and others safe. Crying and showing weakness in front of others cost me my last job, and it was something I was *never* going to let happen again. He understood and agreed to keep me informed.

Sadly, on my way home from work the following Tuesday afternoon, I got the phone call I had been dreading. His family decided to take him off life support. I was absolutely devastated. Even though these juveniles are "inmates," they are like our own children in many ways. We do our best to guide them to make better choices, share in the joys of their successes, and feel their disappointments when they fall short. I felt great sadness thinking about how he must have felt so misunderstood and alone—enough to have resorted to taking his own life. He was so young.

We held a memorial service for him in the jail where staff, residents, and even his family attended. It was scheduled on my day off, but I wasn't going to miss it. I needed to be there. At the end of the service conducted by our chaplain, his mother spoke with staff and inmates and received hugs and condolences. I didn't want to face her. Even though there was nothing more that I could have done in that situation, I felt like I failed her. My coworkers who were sitting with me encouraged me to speak to her. Finding the courage, I approached her and gave her a hug. "I'm so sorry for your loss," I told her as I tried to catch my breath between tears. "I was the one who gave him CPR."

I braced myself for her reaction. I was prepared for anger, resentment, or any number of emotions that she would have been justified in feeling.

"I'm sorry that you had to go through that," she said to me, with grace, as she hugged me again, this time even tighter. I couldn't believe this mother, who just lost one of her children, apologized to me for doing my job. I had no words. I went and sat next to my unit manager on the side of the visit room and bowed my head and cried. Shortly after I sat down, the inmate's brother approached us and said, "Because of what you did, the hospital was able to keep him alive long enough to donate his organs." He too, with every reason in the world to be angry or hateful, went out of his way to give me this peace.

My supervisor and I bawled like babies. It was the most powerful gift I've ever received, in spite of such a tragic situation. I will hold on to those words for the rest of my life.

BURNING OUT

After working on the job for a year and a half, I was emotionally and physically exhausted. I often worked double shifts, not always voluntarily. It was common to get notice at 10:30 p.m. that you would not be clocking out as planned but staying until 6:45 a.m. because we were shorthanded. Staffing would stabilize for short periods, but there were so many vacancies that many of us worked overtime on a regular basis.

For a long time, I kept going because I felt I could make a difference. After about a year and a half on the job, however, I no longer believed I could redirect these kids to more productive lives. Even the best-behaved kids would resort back to their criminal behaviors and flee once they were given off-grounds privileges. We witnessed this fall from grace so many times that watching them start back at square one over and over again was depressing.

I was burning out, and it started to show. One Saturday evening, three kids destroyed everything in the unit they could get their hands on. They threw trash cans filled with leftover food (this time, chili and refried beans) and other stinky garbage. They threw chairs and destroyed furniture. And they popped sprinklers in both pods. To prevent pipes from freezing during winter, our sprinkler system also ran oil through them. That meant that whenever a sprinkler head was tampered with, water wasn't the only substance spewing everywhere. While the inmates who popped the sprinklers didn't care about what got destroyed, other inmates did. So, in addition to trying to maintain some sort of authority over the unruly inmates and preventing them from destroying anything else, I also had to keep the peace among those who were getting rightfully pissed that the few valuables they had were getting destroyed by the oily, mucky water. Once everyone was safely dealt with and placed on lockdown, the staff was in charge of clean up. I grew tired of scrubbing chili off the walls, stuffing trash bags, and using the industrial-sized wet vac to suck up the gallons of water sprayed about the place. The unit was always a mess, and there was nothing I could do but continue cleaning it up, only to do it all over again the next day since no one ever suffered any consequences. This level of chaos had been commonplace on the weekend shift for months—so much so that the administration started working weekends to shadow the units and witness the chaos firsthand.

Not that it helped. Nothing changed afterward.

Juvenile facilities are not like adult facilities. As staff, our options regarding force and restriction were severely limited. As such, we couldn't deploy a lot of the same measures you'd find at adult facilities. For example, we were required to run through every possible option before physically restraining an inmate. This usually included verbal commands and "negotiating." We were prohibited from using pepper spray, even though it is an effective, nonlethal tool. We also didn't have restraint chairs or twenty-four-hour lockdowns. Studies show that isolation for long periods of time is detrimental to mental health, so we didn't do that for a juvenile inmate's well-being. Everything we did was meant to be in the best interest of the juvenile. After all, we were trying to rehab and "save" these young souls from a life of crime.

As a result, we resorted to bargaining with inmates to meet our demands. And even then, it wasn't an "our way or the highway" approach; committed inmates who continued arguing often exhausted staff into submitting to their requests.

I grew so frustrated with the system that I often couldn't contain myself. On several occasions, I completely broke down and lost my composure on other staff members who consistently cut my legs out from under me—and that's putting it nicely!

While the intention of the juvenile facility was to help these young inmates improve their lives, it didn't work. The system was too soft on them, and as a result, it only encouraged these criminals to see what they could get away with. In adult facilities, rules are rules. There are no ifs, ands, or buts if an adult inmate steps out of line, regardless of how small the incident. If you did X, you suffered Y consequences—period (which usually meant additional charges with significant increases on their sentences). There is no discussion, and definitely no bargaining.

At a juvenile facility, however, rules were routinely bent, if not outright broken. There was zero follow-through from administrators and staff. And what does that teach young criminals? It certainly doesn't teach them respect, or accountability, or that their actions have consequences. It teaches them to push the boundaries to see if they can come out on top. It encourages them to manipulate. It teaches them to be better criminals.

The sad reality is that our facility didn't deter these inmates from criminal behavior once they completed their program. More often than not, they'd violate one of their conditions and get sent back to jail. Some would get convicted on new charges, usually more violent than before. In my time at the jail, out of every five inmates released, I saw four of them come back.

Everything seemed backward. We should have been harder on these younger minds to strategically and effectively deter them away from a life of crime. And being harder on them doesn't mean being mean or harsh. You can still have a rehabilitative objective and offer support while putting a higher priority on enforcing rules and consequences. Juvenile facilities should implement concrete rules—rules that cannot be broken. No ifs, ands, or buts. Unfortunately, the optics of that does not fly on a political level. The reality is that no commissioner would put his career on the line by proposing the use of pepper spray at a juvenile facility. He'd be ostracized. The public views juveniles as babies, so we must treat them as such. The public seems to forget that many of them are in jail for violent crimes.

The least the juvenile facility could do is enforce its own rules and policies—regardless of how trivial they may seem. For example, we had a building policy (meaning that it applied to all units) that required each inmate to be in uniform before leaving their unit for the day. This meant inmates had to tuck in their shirts and properly strap their shoes. When they walked down hallways, they were supposed to walk with their hands clasped behind their back, in silence; no talking was allowed when walking from point A to point B.

Did this ever happen? Ha! Each unit saw varying degrees of disregard—unless, of course, you were in my unit. Our kids never left the unit until they were in proper uniform. We followed the rules. The inmates in other units, however, individualized their appearances, whether that was tucking their pant legs into their socks, undoing their straps, or not tucking in their shirt. They were rarely quiet in the hallways, and they never walked with their hands clasped behind their back. Each unit implemented and enforced its own set of rules; the building's policy acted only as a guideline. Some units were worse than others, depending on how lax the staff had become. If the whole building ran the same, meaning if the rules were applied evenhandedly throughout all units, things would have been *so much* better. But instead, when the kids got into trouble, they knew they could get somebody from one of the more relaxed units to come and they'd get their way.

And that was the worst: when my colleagues got soft and gave in to requests—especially after I stood my ground and attempted to enforce the rules.

For example, one night over the weekend (of course), a code was called that initiated a lockdown. Three inmates in my unit, however, refused to go to their cells. Instead, they thought it would be a good idea to destroy everything in one of the pods. They started throwing and breaking the plastic chairs into shards to be used as weapons. They tore off the metal cages around the fire alarms. They threw the DVD player across the room, shattering it into pieces.

"Hey!" I screamed from the dayroom. The inmates were locked behind a pod door. I knew they weren't being malicious, just defiant. "You know the drill. Are you guys going to lock down?"

"Yeah, okay, Plante. Are you still going to write us for not locking down?" one of them asked.

"Obviously," I responded. Failing to lock down was a major violation.

Well, that wasn't the answer they were looking for, so they continued their defiant behavior and refused to lock down. I had done this dance so many times before that I instinctually started phoning other units to assemble a team. I was not in the business of negotiating. If I asked them to lock down once and they refused, they would be physically placed in their rooms or escorted to the SMU for the rest of the night. Period.

For some reason, an upper-level administrator was still in the building and, upon hearing the commotion, decided to pop into the unit. "What's going on?" he asked.

"I have three inmates refusing to go to their rooms," I responded, as they continued to trash the pod. He then opened the door to the pod and asked: "What's it going to take for you guys to lock down?"

"Don't write us up!" they replied cheekily.

"That's it?" the administrator replied. "Done deal. Now go to your rooms." And they did.

I was so pissed, I'm sure my face was bright red. If I wanted to follow the path of least resistance, I could have done the same. I could have thrown out all of the rules to make life easier for myself. But I didn't. It was not the way my unit manager wanted his unit to be run, and it wasn't the way I wanted it to be run, either.

As frustrated as I became with the system and our lack of follow-through, I didn't quit; I was still working on my plan. This was just a temporary stepping-stone for me. I was determined to put in five years on the job before I applied for federal positions. *A year and a half done; three and a half more to go.* I also had to complete my master's degree in criminal justice. My goal was to get the inmates in bed by 9:30 p.m. each night so I could pull out my textbook and read about victimology, criminology, rehabilitation, organized crime, and research methods. It was fascinating, because I could draw so many connections to my work. I read about what leads to criminal behavior, biologically and environmentally, and I'd see that information reflected every day in the inmates' actions and behaviors. As hard as I studied, though, I'd have to break routinely for a unit check, but I was determined to make every minute count.

Little did I know how precious those minutes of studying between unit checks were; my life was about to drastically change forever when I found myself caught between a concrete wall and an enraged inmate.

CHAPTER THREE

||||||||||||||||||||||

ASSAULT AND AFTERMATH

The night of the assault started like any other Saturday.

I'd been working the high-risk unit since 2 p.m., and I had enjoyed a relatively manageable day, for our standards, at least. It was never as calm as a classroom or anything—our group of adolescents was always on edge about something.

The inmates in my unit weren't just high-risk; they were also high-needs. Walking around the dayroom, you were face-to-face with the most dangerous juveniles in the entire state. What made them the most dangerous was not their extensive criminal record, or even their history of violence toward staff and other residents, but their unpredictability. And what made them largely unpredictable was the array of mental-health issues that impacted them in one way or another.

The boys ranged in age from fourteen to twenty, and each individual in my unit had a story, a background, and personal experiences that contributed to the behaviors they exhibited. Some inmates had survived abusive upbringings, incarcerated parents, and other horrors too numerous to mention. As a result, some residents struggled with anxiety, depression, post-traumatic stress disorder (PTSD), schizophrenia, and complications related to fetal alcohol syndrome or fetal substance abuse syndrome. The inmates who were exposed to substances prior to birth had severe cognitive delays, which often resulted in difficulty regulating emotions and violent outbursts. Something as simple as a sentence, a word, a look, or even a tone of voice could result in an inmate lashing out in uncontrollable rage.

On the night of the assault, the atmosphere in the unit wasn't exactly mellow, but I didn't sense any unusual tension in the air, either. We had a reasonably relaxed afternoon, a peaceful dinner hour, and then everyone burned off steam at the gym before bed. There were only a handful of residents left behind in the unit with me—most of them watching TV or working on a jigsaw puzzle in the dayroom. We didn't have much longer to go until everyone was tucked in for the night. I watched the clock slowly tick by.

POWDER KEG

I was the only staff member permanently assigned to the high-risk unit on the weekends, so I was in my usual spot at the staff desk in the dayroom. From this vantage point, I could see everything that was happening. I also had access to the control panel that locked and unlocked all the doors, including the pods on either side.

On the shift with me that night was a newer staff member I wasn't too impressed with—he wasn't skilled at building rapport with the inmates and seemed slow to act when things got rough. We were on our own in the unit this weekend; none of the administrators were shadowing, so no serious punishments would be issued until Monday, and the inmates knew it. I went in every Friday night ready for a rodeo, hoping it would be limited to the usual antics like pulling fire alarms, setting off sprinklers, and throwing food. Whatever happened, it would be chaos; you just had to be ready for anything.

Most new staff members started on the weekend shift, but finding someone who could hold their own in this high-risk unit was incredibly challenging. Like many jail facilities, we also suffered from a high turnover rate; nearly half of our new hires would find a new job within a year. As such, staff rotated around quite a bit, especially in the high-risk unit because most people didn't want to work with these kids. New staff could also be easily manipulated by some of the savvier criminals, so we had to watch out for that as well. Since I was specifically assigned to this unit, meaning that I did not rotate to other units, and because I'd been with these kids for more than a year, I was the senior staff on my shift.

I kept a close eye on everyone, but I didn't let one young man out of my sight for a second—a twenty-year-old who had one more year on his sentence for a Class A felony (Class A felonies are severe, high-ranking crimes like murder, armed robbery, rape, and burglary, to name a few). He bragged about mutilating animals while he was high on drugs. He openly fantasized about mass shootings against a specific race of people and then laughed about it. He enjoyed watching other people suffer and had no regard for their pain. He didn't always come off as cold-blooded, though—even though he was. He was a master manipulator. It benefited him when the unit ran well, so he would often act like a model inmate. He led the unit by example and kept the behavior of other residents in check if things started getting out of hand, mostly to get something out of it—like more gym time, for example. As he neared closer to his release, he had even demonstrated enough good behavior to obtain employment outside of the facility.

Not surprisingly, his good behavior didn't last long.

Despite nearing his discharge date, this inmate ran away

from his community job site and went missing. Officials finally caught him five days later. After that escape, he should have landed in county jail with adults, but his lawyer got the charges bumped down to a misdemeanor. After his month-long stint in county waiting for his sentencing, he returned to the juvenile facility with a chip on his shoulder. He acted like he was untouchable. He just beat a charge that should have landed him years in an adult facility. In my unit of boys, all of them younger, this guy had some power. He was incredibly intelligent, manipulative, and intimidating to the other inmates. He would often make bets with the younger kids to extort food from their canteen accounts, or he'd get their meals in dining as payments for any debts. He didn't always take people's food because they owed him; sometimes he did it just because he could. He was quick to make threats, and nobody doubted his ability to follow through on them. They were scared.

Some inmates described him as the "Pod Father"—clearly a joke since there was nothing fatherly about him. But he ran the show; there was no doubt about that.

Upon his arrival the second time around, Pod Father made demands, not requests. For good behavior, staff members could reward residents with luxuries like an extra snack or allow them to stay up past their scheduled bedtime to finish a movie. Pod Father demanded such luxuries. He'd demand extra food or a later bedtime daily. Since his behavior was deplorable at best, his requests were continuously met with firm no's. Because I was the senior staff member on this unit, there was no one inside the unit who could overrule me—which totally pissed him off. He also knew better than to cause a code and get a building supervisor involved—he didn't want to put himself in a position to get any additional write-ups or charges.

"You can give me what I want, or I'm going to make your life a living hell," he told me after I wouldn't give in to one of his demands.

"Send it," I replied sternly. He wasn't going to intimidate me. This was *my* unit.

He meant his words, though. He was determined to get me kicked off the unit. He started by recruiting a fourteen-year-old resident to make allegations against me, which usually dictated that the staff member be removed from the unit until the investigation was completed. If I wasn't in this unit on the weekends, however, the unit would be run by brand-new staff who could be easily manipulated into doing things that weren't usually allowed. Fortunately, my unit manager was aware of the motives driving these allegations and refused to let the inmates dictate who was going to run the unit. To avoid utter anarchy, he stuck his neck out to keep me on the unit while I was formally investigated, which only lasted a couple of weeks. The fourteen-year-old who made the allegations eventually admitted that he lied, and that he was put up to it, even though he wouldn't say by whom (we all knew).

As everyone came back into the dayroom after gym time that Saturday, the vibe was fairly laid-back. The inmates who stayed behind to watch TV or work a puzzle were happy they got some quiet time, and the gym rats were happy they got a workout. The dinner trays were cleared, and the kids settled into the couches in front of me to watch a movie. I was thrilled to have a period of relative calm before the bedtime chaos started with cries of "I can't find my clothes," "Where is my towel?" and "I don't have any socks!" How this happened every day was beyond me; they each had four of everything, with their names ironed on them (like a name tag), and their laundry was done five days a week.

For the moment, everything seemed as calm and controlled as it ever did, until I heard one kid yell, "I'm going to kill myself."

The statement came out of the blue. He didn't sound upset or distraught; it was like he was stating a fact. Everyone knew that signaling suicidal intent required us to assign a dedicated staff member to their care, so I assigned my coworker as his one-on-one and grabbed the clipboard to document the incident. I was now the only staff member responsible for the group as a whole, so I made the decision to lock down the unit. The inmates knew that this protocol would come as soon as the inmate made his statement. When I called the lock down and cycled the doors, the inmates started walking themselves to their rooms. After all, we did this at least five times during any given weekend, so they had it pretty down pat.

I stood at the staff desk, watching everyone make their way to the pod doors on each side of the dayroom. Each inmate had his own room, which was located in one of two pods. Each pod was a big square, similar in size to the dayroom, with a big open area in the middle. Around the perimeter of each pod were the inmate rooms.

I looked to my right at the B-Pod, which had twelve rooms. Once all of the inmates entered the pod and headed toward their individual rooms, the pod door closed and locked behind them. Once they entered their own rooms, those doors locked behind them as well. Once those residents were secured behind the B-Pod door, I turned my attention to the A-Pod door. The other unit staff member was following the inmate who made the suicidal statements toward the pod door. He dragged his feet, walking slow enough to let the other residents walk past him into the pod first as they headed to their individual rooms. When he reached the door to the A-Pod, however, he let the door close in front of him, leaving him in the dayroom.

At this point, fifteen inmates were secured behind at least one locked door, and one was not.

As soon as that pod door locked, that inmate turned around and started walking toward me. He started yelling as he scooped some puzzle pieces from the table beside the desk and threw them in my face.

What the hell? What is this guy doing? Everything was going so smoothly, and now this? I called a code for assistance, stating an inmate was throwing items at staff. The tone in my voice broke while I made the call. I was getting pissed, and things were escalating quickly. I did not understand why this inmate's outburst was directed at me, or what provoked it.

"Stop!" I yelled. I could hear my tone crack with anger as he threw another cup of pieces at my face. My rage broke through the professionalism I was trying to maintain. Trying to be the "bigger person" in a physical situation where I was not the bigger person was a dangerous game that I did not want to play. But fight or flight was kicking in, and I wasn't going anywhere. My instincts told me to stand my ground.

After there were no more puzzle pieces to throw, he picked up one of the plastic chairs and threw it in my direction. He missed. When he picked up the second chair to throw at me, I met him halfway and grabbed onto it. With my adrenaline building, I pushed that chair back into him with everything I had. Meanwhile, my fellow staff member—a former college football player who constantly bragged about his accolades—stood just feet behind him, doing absolutely nothing. This inmate had at least six inches and probably one hundred pounds on me. If a staff member ever got assaulted, you were supposed to do whatever necessary to protect your fellow staff members. He could have done a multitude of things to assist me, like tackle the inmate to the ground or wrap his arms around his torso from behind. But he didn't. He just stood there. People like him were the reason why I always trained as hard as I did. I made sure I could take care of myself, because when it matters most, you can't count on anybody but yourself.

I managed to remove the chair from the situation, leaving just the two of us, face-to-face. That's when his fists came up. I immediately ducked my head down; one square hit would be lights out for me. When I ducked, he managed to get me into a headlock and started dropping hammer fists to the top of my head over, and over, and over again.

Bam! Bam! Bam! Bam!

I barely registered the blows. I didn't feel any pain. I only felt his anger, and how badly he wanted to hurt me. I had spent much of my life fighting competitively in various forms of martial arts, so I understood the severity of being held in a choke hold. Any position involving a choke hold is considered a deadly force situation, meaning the potential for death is much higher compared to other situations. I had to get out. Although I knew how to punch and kick, I was not in a position to deliver any significant blows, and I doubted that he would feel them anyway due to his own adrenaline rush.

Being put in a choke provided my coworker with a "no holds barred" opportunity to intervene in any way possible to assist me, but he continued to stand there doing nothing.

As I tried to figure a way out, my training about what to do in a choke hold came back to me in a flash: go for the groin. I lunged, grabbed, twisted, and tried to get hold of anything I could so he would let me go.

It worked.

He stopped throwing punches and released his hold of me, dropping me to the ground. It was over. After he let me go, I watched as he casually walked toward the unit door heading to the SMU. The other staff member casually walked next to him and led him out the front door of the unit as if nothing had happened.

I was left alone, stunned, enraged, my hair tangled all

around my face, when a responding staff member from the girls' unit came in through the back door. It had probably only taken him seconds to run from the girls' unit to my door, but it felt significantly longer.

"Where is he?" was the first question out of his mouth. I pointed to the hallway. "Get him on the ground," I heard him shout. "He just assaulted staff! Get him in handcuffs!"

It took six staff members to get the inmate restrained and moved to the SMU, and I heard him screaming crude insults in my direction the whole time. I've heard a lot of cursing in the unit, but this was different; it felt extremely personal, and I had no idea why. I hadn't done anything to provoke this. I knew this kid, too. Yes, he had a hair-trigger temper, but even this was strangely out of character for him. We'd developed a good rapport with each other, and I would have known if he had an issue with me before this situation erupted.

Something just didn't add up.

SHELL-SHOCKED

After my assailant was dragged away kicking and screaming, I resumed my job responsibilities as if nothing happened. *Just another day on the job*, I told myself. I walked around to each inmate's door and pulled the handles to make sure they were securely locked. As I walked each pod, I fielded questions the kids were yelling from their rooms, as they could see that my hair was no longer in a tight bun.

"Plante, what happened?"

"Did you get hit?"

I gave brief, basic answers; I was all business. Some of them couldn't see what happened from their rooms, but they heard the commotion and were genuinely concerned. Others, unfortunately, did witness it and had strong reactions to it. One inmate later confided in another staff member: "I hadn't seen a woman get beaten that bad since I watched my dad beat my mom." These juveniles might be criminals from all walks of life, but the one thing the majority of them agreed on is that you *never* hit a woman. Many of those inmates would have intervened, more than my coworker had, if they hadn't been locked in their rooms.

After making sure the unit was secure, I started documenting the incident and completing the appropriate paperwork to transfer that inmate to the SMU. To make sure my reporting of the assault was accurate, I reviewed the security video.

The video was confusing—it didn't match my memory. I thought I got knocked to the ground at the end, but apparently, I was standing the whole time. I never actually fell to the floor, but in my mind, I had sat there watching him walk across the dayroom. I also couldn't exactly recall how many times he hit me. My best guess was that it was somewhere between ten and twenty times. Since the video didn't record continually, I only saw what happened in two-to-three-second intervals, so we couldn't accurately count the blows. In one clip, you can see him approaching me, the next clip showed him three feet closer, and then there were three clips of him on top of me. My bottom lip was also split and swollen, but I didn't remember getting hit in the face. The disconnect was unsettling; it was as if my brain was protecting me from processing the worst parts of the assault.

I ignored the violence itself and fixated on the coworker's role. In the security video, I saw the other staff member standing behind the inmate while I was being assaulted, but he was just waving his arms around, not actually intervening. Multiple complaints had been made about this staff member by unit managers throughout the building, yet he was assigned to work on a high-risk unit? He shouldn't have even been in the building, but here he was, probably because he was a former college football player who looked like he could put anyone down. He never did. Hell, I had broken up more fights than he had. Everyone else who watched the video agreed—he was utterly useless.

Oddly, I wasn't angry with my assailant. I had a gut feeling it wasn't his idea and that he had been put up to it. I also had a pretty good idea of who the instigator was. I understood that this younger kid was more scared of the Pod Father than of me, so he likely felt he had no choice but to do his bidding.

In the meantime, with the unit locked down for the night, I heated my Buffalo Wild Wings leftovers in the staff bubble and sat down to eat. I tuned out the constant buzzing from the pods; the ringleader who I suspected started this whole thing was calling out to us endlessly, and everybody else wanted out of lockdown, too, so they were pressing the buzzers in their rooms. Staff from other units had arrived to help at this point, so I let them handle the residents while I started typing my report.

Twenty minutes later, two supervisors, a man and a woman, came in with concerned looks on their faces. "Are you okay?" they asked me, with an urgency that surprised me.

"Oh, yeah, I'm fine. I'm just chilling. Eating my dinner."

"Well, we should take you over to medical," said the woman.

"Oh, no, it's fine," I insisted. It didn't seem like a big deal to me. But I knew this was protocol, so I reluctantly did as I was instructed. My supervisors took over, taking pictures of the injuries to my face and sending me to medical. I figured I would get the formalities over so I could get back to work.

Little did I know, this night was far from over.

|||||||||||||||||||||||||

CHAPTER FOUR

INVISIBLE INJURY

Being in the medical unit was a little like being in a fish-bowl—the windows are huge and the doors are transparent, so anyone walking by can see you standing at the front desk. This made me uncomfortable. If word got around to the inmates that I was injured, it could be exploited. Any sign of vulnerability could put me at further risk.

I was friendly with the nursing staff, so I chatted with them as they did all the standard things, like taking my temperature and checking my vitals. They had been working in the building longer than I had, and we often saw each other several times during a shift.

Our nursing staff was almost as much on the front lines as we were. There was rarely an incident inside the facility that they weren't involved in at one point or another. The nurses were responsible for distributing medications to all of the inmates in the building three times a day, evaluating inmates who submitted "sick call" slips before seeing a doctor, and medically overseeing new intakes (new residents) and suicide watches. Those, however, were the easier parts of their job. They often were the first responders to suicide attempts, emergency situations like the swallowing of batteries, and vicious fights that resulted in broken bones. They worked equally as hard as we did—and were equally as underappreciated.

As they evaluated me, I told them what happened. As my adrenaline started to wear off, I felt a pain in my left shoulder. The nurses took a quick look at it, but didn't see anything out of the ordinary. I figured my muscles would be sore for a few days, shook it off, and went back to man my unit. I had to keep up appearances to let the inmates know that I was still there.

I had to make it clear—to one inmate in particular—that they couldn't get rid of me that easily.

When I returned to my unit a half hour later, it was still unusually chaotic. When lockdowns occur near bedtime, most residents accept they will be in their rooms for the rest of the night and go to sleep. Not tonight, apparently. Everyone was still up and rowdy. As I walked by the control panel, I heard room B-9 making the most racket. The inmate kept buzzing continuously, requesting to be let out.

Of course this room was the loudest one. It belonged to the Pod Father.

As other staff went to his door, I heard him making demands through the microphone. It was already 9 p.m., though, so it was lights out. We were not coming off of lockdown, and nobody was coming out of their rooms—period. This didn't please the Pod Father, and he continued demanding he be let out. When we refused, he requested a grievance form. A grievance form was a way to complain about mistreatment of inmates, by staff or by fellow inmates. This inmate always harassed other residents who filled out these forms because he considered it a form of "snitching," something unforgivable in his mind. And here he was, filling one out. What a hypocrite!

The hypocrisy was actually a red flag since it was so out of character. He was trying to exert power over me by getting his way after he made his move—but that certainly was not going to happen.

As I watched this young man continually try to manipulate the staff and our system, I couldn't believe the sharp decline in his mental state and his behavior since returning to our facility. His manipulation tactics were through the roof. I also couldn't believe he was allowed to return to this juvenile facility with no additional time on his sentence after what he'd done.

But I guess I shouldn't have been *that* surprised. The juvenile correctional system had plenty of issues itself. Every decision that was made had a political agenda. The judges, the lawyers, and the facility directors only cared about the following:

1. **Maintaining good appearances.** In an attempt to appear proactive and like we were making a difference, many incarcerated offenders had their sentences shortened and were released before they were ready, so our numbers would look good on paper.
2. **Avoiding negative press.** You weren't going to see any news about officer assaults in our local paper, or of prisoners escaping from our facility. You certainly wouldn't see any comments from the commissioner, either.
3. **Reducing recidivism statistics.** This was done strategically by refusing to charge juveniles despite multiple arrests.

What are missing from this list are staff safety, inmate safety, and effective policies and procedures. We as staff knew that these people didn't care about us; we knew they were only out for themselves. In this situation, allowing this incredibly dangerous individual to return to a juvenile facility was by far the most damaging decision they made—not only to me, but also to the other residents in my unit whom I was expected to protect. They released a fox into a locked hen house.

I let the other staff members deal with the rowdy teenagers as I returned to the staff bubble to finish submitting the initial report. But the longer I stayed, the worse I felt.

When my supervisors initially came to my unit after the assault, they had suggested I go to the emergency room at the nearby hospital. Staff often sustained broken noses and concussions that needed to be evaluated by outside medical professionals, but I certainly didn't want to go, not with all my inmates' eyes on me.

"I'll go to the ER once my shift is over at 10:30," I told them. "I'll go once all my inmates are asleep."

Despite how determined I was to make it to the end of my shift, and only having a little over an hour to go, something wasn't right. Physically, the pain in my shoulder grew worse and worse by the minute. It was too painful to move—even a little. Mentally, I started to feel pretty out of it, like I was in a mental fog, or daydreaming. I felt off. When my supervisors returned to check in on me, I told them that I was ready to go to the hospital. Most of my inmates had gone to bed at that point, which made me feel good. I would be back in the morning without them ever knowing I had left.

ER VISIT

Situated in the middle of a city, on a Saturday night at 10

p.m., the emergency room was the last place I wanted to be. It was going to be a long night. Still in my uniform, I gave one clinician after another an account of the assault, which I hated doing. It made me feel weak. I didn't want others to think someone else got the best of me. But I tucked away my ego and repeated the story. I felt so awful.

After what felt like an hour of sitting in the waiting area, my name was finally called and I was escorted to be seen. As I suspected, the ER was packed with people. As we walked, the nurse pointed me toward one of the gurneys that was set up in the hallway.

Oh no—absolutely not, I thought to myself. *There is no way I'm going to sit here in the middle of a hallway for the entire world to see.* This night couldn't get any worse.

"I'll just stand here," I told the nurse, refusing to sit on the gurney.

As I waited to be seen by the doctor, my shoulder hurt worse than ever, and I started to feel queasy. Something was going on with my vision, too—the whole world looked a little cloudy. Begrudgingly, I finally gave in and sat on that gurney. I might have bigger issues to deal with than how I looked to strangers.

It was finally my turn to see the doctor. I repeated the chain of events of the assault for what felt like the tenth time that night. I was concerned that he might not take my concerns as seriously because my situation wasn't as critical as some of the other patients in the ER, but fortunately, he was very kind and attentive. He scrutinized every inch of me like I was the only patient on his schedule. He checked my eyes and how they moved, the strength and ability to move my arms, among other diagnostic tests.

"That shoulder," he finally said. "Let's get it X-rayed."

An X-ray? I thought. *What's that going to show? Didn't I just pull some muscles?*

An hour later, the doctor returned with the results. When he showed me the films, I was stunned. There was an inch-wide gap between my clavicle and my shoulder blade.

"You have an AC separation, third degree," the doctor announced. "We're going to put you in a sling for twelve weeks."

Twelve weeks in a sling? That's going to pose a problem at work. Even so, I felt validated that at least there was something legitimately wrong and I wasn't just being a big baby about the whole thing.

"You also appear to have a severe concussion," the doctor

continued. "You'll need to remain in a dark room to give yourself time to heal. No phone, no television, no computer, and no driving for two weeks." I was fitted with a sling and handed discharge papers. I was still in disbelief. I felt pretty disconnected—like the entire night had been a bad dream.

I guess I wasn't going back to work in the morning like I had planned.

GROUNDED

I've been working eighty-hour weeks; I could use a two-week vacation, I thought to myself as I drove home from the ER. *I'll just take a few weeks off, get refreshed, and get back to work.*

I heard the doctor's words, but I didn't really absorb them in a way most other people would. I know this sounds absurd, but I honestly did not think what happened to me was a big deal, even after the doctor showed me the gap in my shoulder.

It wasn't the first time I was hit by an inmate on the job, although it was the first male. I intervened in several fights and restraints with both male and female inmates, but was always able to neutralize the inmate before any significant punches were thrown my way. Fights broke out at our facility all the time, so my assault didn't seem like a big deal. I didn't think I was invincible or anything, but thanks to all my training, I thought I could protect myself from sustaining any significant injuries. And yet, here I was with my arm in my sling. As I rode home, I felt a little chink in my armor.

By the following morning, that armor fell off entirely when pain like nothing I'd ever experienced before woke me out of a dead sleep. My head hurt so much, I couldn't even open my eyes. The pressure in my head was so intense, it felt like my skull was about to explode. This was not the way the doctor explained concussions to me. He had said I'd be sensitive to light and sound, and to stay in a dark room and chill out. But wow. This was something else. My entire body ached, like I had been run over by a truck—maybe even two or three.

There was no way I was going anywhere.

Not only did my body feel like I'd been in a train wreck, but within a few days, I started to have noticeable problems with my speech and struggled with speaking. I knew what I wanted to say, but I couldn't physically get the words out. When I started, I'd often get halfway through a sentence before completely forgetting what I was talking about. I've always thought of myself as an articulate person, so not being able to communicate a simple thought brought me to tears. I was so frustrated, and there was nothing I could do about it.

It was one thing to be physically injured; most physical injuries have a treatment plan and prognosis and would usually heal with time. My brain injury, however, was a whole new ball game. I had always thought concussions were "no big deal," but this experience changed my tune. For the first time in my life, I felt incredibly stupid, and for me, that was worse than any of my other injuries. I didn't know much about brain injuries at the time, so I didn't know if I would struggle with speaking temporarily or if this was going to be the new normal.

I also noticed changes with my emotional regulation. I cried a lot more often, which according to my physician wasn't out of the ordinary. He told me that head injuries often cause various challenges with regulating emotions.

For at least two weeks, maybe a month, the pain and pressure in my head were relentless and completely debilitating. All I wanted to do was sleep, because it was too painful even to open my eyes, but the pain was so intense that it kept me from sleeping. My depth perception was off, too, so if I got out of bed, I moved slowly and carefully. Every time I walked downstairs, I gripped the rail for dear life, tracing the steps with my feet to get my bearings.

At the same time, I was incredibly restless. I couldn't even sit and watch TV when I was finally allowed to. If I sat down at all, I'd stand back up. I was so agitated; I couldn't have stayed sitting if someone had tied me to a chair.

Even though I couldn't sleep, walk, or talk, and despite feeling constant pain, I stubbornly refused to accept my situation. *I just need to heal so I can get back to my life.* After about a week, I tried to push my recovery by driving to the grocery store down the road—which was a huge mistake. But it was during this drive that I finally got an appreciation for the severity of the damage that had been done to my brain.

As I drove down the road, I could see when cars approached from side streets, when streetlights changed colors, and when drivers changed lanes, but my brain did not process any of it. It felt like my brain was on a five-second delay. I could see things as they happened, but I couldn't register if other people were going to stop, if the light was going to change, or if someone was going to pull out in front of me.

I was utterly terrified. My brain injury was no joke, and it took me attempting to drive to fully drive that message home. It wasn't just a punch in the face. It wasn't just a bloody lip. This was serious. I finally acknowledged that my injury was significant and that it wasn't something I could shake off in a few days.

If I wanted to get better, I needed to prioritize my recovery. My doctor only prescribed two weeks in a dark room with no stimuli for my concussion, so that's what I did. He said the brain would heal itself over time. Once I started physical therapy for my shoulder, I figured the exercises would benefit and help heal my brain, too. We started each session with cardio, which increases the blood flow to your body, including the brain. All I needed to do was give my body time and let it heal itself.

A VICIOUS CYCLE

As my strength slowly returned over the next few months, I tried doing more of my usual things, like hiking in the woods with a friend. Unfortunately, anything that involved a lot of visual stimuli brought the migraines back a hundred times worse. Each time I tried to regain some normalcy, it would knock me back to square one. This happened three times. I felt as if every time I took one step forward, I fell three steps back.

I didn't understand. I was doing everything I was told, yet no matter what I did or how hard I tried, I was caught in this vicious cycle. It was slowly breaking my spirits.

I thought going back to work would help me feel better and give me something else to focus on. I'd worked my whole life, often working two jobs and an internship at the same time; working was what I did—it was part of my identity. After a few weeks of physical therapy, I was eager to return to work, if only in a limited capacity. When other employees were injured at work, they were usually given easy assignments in the lobby or control room, or even just filing paperwork in our maintenance building outside of the facility. I was willing to take one of these "light duty" positions, despite my debilitating headaches.

When I asked my employer about a "light duty" position, they informed me that their policy had since changed: they were no longer offering any "light duty" positions. Their new policy required returning employees to be medically cleared at 100 percent by a doctor before returning to the secured perimeter.

I was a long way from 100 percent.

The isolation of being home all the time slowly started to eat away at me. I was determined to get my life back on track in one way or another. *If they won't let me work in my condition,* I told myself, *then I'll just find somewhere else to work.*

I went to interviews with my arm in a sling and tried to answer interview questions intelligently, even though my language processing was not fully back online. In fact, articulating responses proved to be incredibly difficult. I did my best to remember all the parts to a question, and then answer without losing my train of thought. Unfortunately, I asked them to repeat their questions several times, because as hard as I tried, I kept losing my words.

Needless to say, I didn't get any job offers.

Despite my determination to get better, my condition only continued to decline. I saw my doctor on almost a weekly basis to check in for my Workers' Comp evaluation, and after a month, there was nearly no improvement with my symptoms.

"You're likely suffering from post-concussion syndrome, Derryen," my doctor explained to me. "Unfortunately, I don't know how long this could last. It could take weeks, months, or even years."

Years? I couldn't wrap my head around suffering like this for years, but there was nothing to be done. I essentially just had to wait it out and let my brain heal itself. In the meantime, I kept doing everything they asked me to do, like physical therapy. Eager to help my recovery along as quickly as possible, I looked forward to the session and welcomed the various drills. As a former athlete, I thought I knew what to expect: the exercises would be hard at first, but I'd get better at them each time. Before long, I'd master them, right? Wrong. Simple balance exercises that should have been easy for me as a former cheerleader were, in fact, incredibly difficult.

True to form, the failures only made me push myself harder. I'd been working this way since I was a little girl and it had always paid off: I'd push a little harder and I'd reach my goal. If the therapist told me to do two sets of ten, I'd do two sets of fifteen. If she told me it would take six months, I'd aim for four. Tenacity helped a little bit with strength training, mainly because I started with such low weights, so I was bound to make progress. But with balance exercises, I couldn't change the result no matter how much I practiced, and that cut me to the core. I was the girl who always wanted to perform to the highest standard. This was who I was. Wasn't hard work the recipe for success?

July passed.

Then August.

Still, no improvement.

I was mystified. I didn't understand it at the time, but there was literally no way I could have pushed hard enough to succeed, because we weren't addressing the real issue. We weren't looking in the right places. I did a lot of exercises to strengthen my shoulder, but nobody did any brain scans. The head-injury part of this picture was invisible to everyone but me.

I knew it was there. I just didn't know what to do about it. I enjoyed small windows of improvement when I would gain some strength and balance, but inevitably, the headaches would come back even worse than before. If I felt slightly better for a few days, I lived in dread of the moment when the migraines and nausea would creep back in.

I was determined to get better, but with each setback, my hope was getting dimmer and dimmer.

BEING SEEN

September proved to be my most challenging month yet. I was more than three months out from my assault and in the worst physical condition to date. Time wasn't healing me like the doctors said it would. It was making me feel worse. The nausea had become so severe that it kept me from eating. I lost about a pound per day during that month. I became so emaciated, I looked and felt like a corpse. I could feel my body deteriorating, as if it was eating away at itself.

The isolation I felt at home was compounded because I kept those around me at arm's length from the start. I didn't even call my parents the night of the assault because I knew they would both be asleep and I didn't want them to wake up in a panic. I called them the next day, but spared them from any details.

There were days when the nausea crippled me so severely, I couldn't fathom getting out of bed. It was so intense that it felt like I had the flu for six weeks. It was hard for close friends and family to be empathetic, but that's because they didn't understand the severity of how I was feeling—often because I didn't tell them. There wasn't much they could do for me even if they did. Hell, there wasn't much that I could do for myself, either. I felt more and more helpless each day. I was approaching my breaking point.

Feeling alone and desperate, I reached out to a former mentor of mine. "I'm having a hard time," I confided in him through text. "I feel so alone—and I am in an unbearable amount of pain. I don't know how much longer I can do this. I can't live like this anymore."

"Promise me you won't do anything to hurt yourself," he texted back. Crickets. I didn't answer him. "Derryen, promise me," he texted again.

"I don't know if I can do that."

A few moments later, I texted him again saying that I was fine. I told him my mom and I were going out for ice cream and that he shouldn't worry about me.

Minutes later, as my mom and I pulled out of the driveway, a police car came around the corner and stopped us. *Oh gosh*, I thought to myself. I knew exactly what was going on, so I got out of the car without even looking at my mother.

"Are you Derryen?" the officer asked me as he approached the car.

"Yes—can we talk in private?" I said.

"We just got a call from someone saying they wanted us to come check on you. Is everything all right, ma'am?"

"I'm fine, officer," I told him. "I am suffering from a brain injury, so things are a little rough, but I'm okay. Thanks for taking the time, sir." I held onto that tough demeanor and got back into the car.

"What was that?" asked my mother. I had kept my mother completely in the dark about my mental struggles, but at this point there was no hiding it anymore.

"Mom," I said in a calm, matter-of-fact tone. "I have lost my will to live. I am in *so* much pain, I just can't do it anymore."

I saw a mix of emotions come and go across her face: anger, fear, helplessness. I could tell she was shocked. She finally realized how severe my situation was. If things had gone differently that day, I might have never told her. If the cop had come when my mother was out, I'm sure she still wouldn't know. But the universe caught me; I couldn't hide it any more.

"Do you want to go to the ER and try to get a brain scan?" she asked.

"No, mom. I've already been. There's nothing they can do."

"There has to be something they could do," she insisted.

"Mom, I'm suffering from post-concussion syndrome. My doctor said there's no prognosis. The ER will be a complete waste of time."

"Well, how about your nausea? The least they could do is give you something for that so you can start eating."

I didn't have the strength to argue, so I agreed. If I could eat again, that would be a start, at least. Then we could try to deal with everything else.

CHAPTER FIVE

IIIIIIIIIIIIIIIIIIIIII

GETTING HELP

Before my mom took me to the ER, I grabbed my pink floral backpack filled with my textbooks. I had discussion posts to write on Tuesdays and Thursdays, quizzes on Fridays, and papers due on Sundays, so I figured I'd read through a couple of chapters in the waiting room. I sat there, high-lighter in hand, studying while waiting to be seen once again by a doctor.

Even though the rest of my life was in chaos, studying for my master's was the one piece of normalcy I clung on to.

After three hours in the waiting room, a nurse finally called my name. I never mentioned my suicidal thoughts to her or anyone else I saw that day. If I had, I knew they would hold me for three days, and my file would then contain the words "psychiatric hospitalization," which I did not want on my record. Instead, I focused on the issues that needed to be addressed.

"I'm recovering from a head injury, but my nausea is so severe, I'm not eating," I told her. "I've lost a lot of weight because of it, and I wanted to see if you could help me with the nausea."

The doctor who treated me came across as though she didn't believe me. From the way she looked at me, to the tone in her voice, I felt like something was off. She looked at me like I was seeking medications, which was the last thing I wanted. I could feel my body withering away every, single, day. I felt so weak. I just wanted to get rid of the nausea, so I could eat.

A few hours later I was discharged with a prescription to an anti-nausea medication. No new tests were done. As relieved as I was at the thought that this might help some of my symptoms, I wished for nothing more than to find out what was causing me so much unbearable pain. Unfortunately, with post-concussion syndrome, there was nothing I could do but suck it up and deal with it. So, I did.

I took the anti-nausea medication immediately—and it worked. The nausea subsided enough for me to eat, and I started to regain some weight.

Even though I wasn't cleared to return to the jail, I was

desperate to return to some form of work. I thought that keeping myself busy and getting out of the isolation would be the best remedy for the depression I was feeling. I had already interviewed for a job as a revenue agent at the state revenue department, so I looked forward to my appointment with a new neurologist, hoping he would at least clear me for that job if I were to get it.

The day of my appointment I was partially hopefully that he would shed some light onto what I was experiencing, too. Maybe he'd see something that the other doctors hadn't, but he didn't. I talked to him about the emotional dysregulation I was experiencing, the severe migraines, the nausea. He evaluated my eyes and came to the same conclusion everyone else had so far: PCS. He offered nothing new for me—no prognosis, no treatment plan. He said the same thing everyone had: "You're just going to have to wait it out." When I asked him about wanting to return to work, he was very frank with me.

"I can't tell you how it's going to work out," he warned me. "You might not be able to do it."

Damn it, I thought to myself. He must have seen the look on my face.

"But I suppose it's worth a try," he said. "I can clear you for work." Before I left, however, he gave me a warning: "You can jump out of the nest, but I'm not guaranteeing you're going to fly."

Finally, a bit of good news, especially since I was offered the job as a revenue agent for the state revenue department, which I gladly accepted.

NEW SURROUNDINGS

The first day on the job was intimidating. It was mid-October, and walking into my new office on my first day was quite a culture shock. Although the atmosphere in the office was considerably laid-back, it was still a far cry from the jail culture I was used to.

I met my new coworkers and was escorted to my new work station. It was a cubicle. This really sent me into shock. Growing up, I swore I would never work a desk job. Working at a desk for hours on end was never a part of my plan. I was meant for the field—dealing with things upfront, getting my hands dirty, using both my body and my mind—and yet here I was: sitting in my own cubicle for the first time. I felt like my career took a step backward.

It was such a drastic change that I thought back fondly to my unit full of problem children. I missed the familiarity, I missed the hands-on environment, and I even missed the inmates. I spent a lot of time with them, building rapport, and doing all I could to help them improve their lives. I wondered what they thought happened to me. One day I was there, and the next day I was gone. It's not like I quit that job. The inmates didn't know that, so I felt guilty for abandoning them. Despite the assault and its traumatic repercussions, positive memories flooded my brain.

Sitting at my new desk, I heard the neurologist's words in my head. *You can jump out of the nest, but I'm not guaranteeing you're going to fly.*

I snapped out of my nostalgia. *This is a fresh start*, I thought. So, like any fledgling, I flapped for all I was worth. The work was very demanding mentally, and there was a significant amount of laws and regulations to learn. I continued to persist through the migraines and to do my best not to let my injury affect me.

As time passed, I realized what a great fit this job was for me. It involved material I was naturally interested in, and it had some criminal justice components. It was as if I was getting the best of both worlds. My senior coworkers were very supportive: they took the time to praise me when I did a good job and to lend an ear when I needed one. Three months into the job, I finally started to feel at home.

At this point, I was able to function day-to-day, and I was thrilled to be bringing in a stable income again. The migraines were still constant, but they seemed more manageable—meaning they reached a seven on the pain scale, rather than a ten. As long as I was busy, I didn't have time to focus on the pain—so naturally, I picked up another job. My desk job was a typical forty-hours-a-week commitment, but I was used to working close to eighty hours at the jail, so I had a lot of extra time on my hands. *I am not going to feel any better if I stay isolated and miserable at home,* I told myself. I blamed my depression on being stuck at home when I wasn't working, so in December, I picked up a second job working a few nights a week at a local restaurant as a waitress. I thought working in a positive environment, feeling productive, and making a few more bucks would help with my recovery process. Why not? I could handle it.

I was back—or at least that's what I told myself. I moved out of my parent's house into an apartment and I was finishing my master's program. My financial situation improved, and I could provide for myself again. I tried to tell myself that was sufficient progress for now, but predictably, when the opportunity came to work a weekend shift at the restaurant, I jumped on it.

Working had always been my coping skill, but by March, I was worn out from working seventy hours a week. Plus, working all the time hadn't helped me escape my symptoms at all; in fact, my migraines crept back to a nine on the pain scale. It felt as if I was waking up with the worst hangover of my life every morning—but drinking Gatorade and eating a banana wasn't a magic cure for these headaches. The pressure in my head was so severe that I had a hard time focusing my vision. Every morning, I sat on the side of the bed for a few minutes before I trusted myself to stand. I knew within the first minutes of waking up what kind of day I was going to have. The pain I woke up with was the pain I endured throughout the rest of the day; it never subsided or got better.

The headaches weren't limited to the mentally straining tasks at work, either; they started becoming more pervasive in other aspects of my life, too—like at family get-togethers, birthday parties, and barbecues. The pain morphed from a constant pressure to a throbbing dagger through the middle of my face, to the point where I would keel over in agony during a flare-up. After a few months of my symptoms being manageable, I was back to square one feeling completely debilitated.

In March, nine months after the assault, I trudged back to the ER. "What brings you in today?" the attending nurse asked.

"I'm have these debilitating migraines, and I want to find out what's causing them," I answered.

"Oh, we won't be able to find that out," he had the nerve

to tell me. "You could have a hole in your heart that could be causing your migraines. It could be anything! We won't be able to figure that out today." I was completely beside myself. It took everything in me not to walk out right then and there, but I didn't. At the end of this visit, no scans, no new advice. "Post-concussion syndrome," they said. "Follow up with your primary," they said.

They offered me pain medications, but I refused them because that was the last thing I wanted. That wasn't what I was there for. I was convinced there was something wrong with me. Something specific. The pain was consistently radiating from the same area: the back of my head right above my spine. I couldn't tell if the doctors didn't believe me, or if they didn't care enough to find out what was actually wrong with me.

I sucked it up for two more months before I was back at the ER again, with next to no expectation of getting help, but with nowhere else to turn. Thank God, this time was different.

When the doctor first came in, I initially got the same vibe that he thought I was a med seeker. He mentioned that I had come in before complaining about the same problem, then asked what had been done about my migraines in previous visits. I shared my story, that I was still having this severe pressure at the base of my skull that hadn't gone away in almost a year.

"What would you like me to do?" he asked.

"Can you just make sure there's nothing physically wrong with my neck? A slipped disk or anything putting pressure at the base of my skull?" I asked.

"Yes," he agreed, "that we can certainly do." I appreciated him giving me the opportunity to express what I felt like I needed and hadn't received during my prior visits. Despite his willingness to help me try to get answers, the scans on my neck showed nothing out of the ordinary. It felt like the last straw. As I sat there trying to take in what he was telling me, my feet dangled over the side of the bed and tears started rolling down my face.

"You know," the doctor said, "I can see that you're really depressed and in a lot of pain. Let me check some things. Hold on a minute."

When he came back, he handed me a couple of business cards. One was for craniosacral therapy, a gentle form of chiropractic that can help reestablish blood flow throughout the brain, and the other for massage therapy.

"These might not fix what is wrong," he said, "but they could help you manage the pain."

I was touched by his gesture. Even if neither of these therapies would help me, it gave me a bit of relief. Here was someone who wasn't doubting me or my pain. He knew it was real and that something was wrong. Even though there was nothing he could do for me, he took the extra step to offer me a couple of options I hadn't explored yet. He gave me something that could offer some comfort—and it did comfort me. I needed all the help I could get.

After my third trip to the ER, I received a phone call from Workers' Compensation.

"We regret to inform you that we will no longer pay for your emergency room bills."

"What?" I said. "I am still in a tremendous amount of pain. What do you mean you won't be covering my ER bills? What am I supposed to do?"

"We are assigning you to a case manager. She will answer all of your questions."

A case manager? Oh, great. Another person to tell me that there was nothing wrong with me, that there was nothing more that could be done, and that this was how I was going to be for the rest of my life? I was not thrilled.

And then I got a phone call from Donna. On the other end of the phone was a woman with a "can do, will do" tone and a list of questions. We ran through the timeline of the treatments I received thus far and what I was experiencing. She started asking me if I had been provided with this evaluation or this test, to which I repeatedly answered no.

"You mean to tell me that they didn't order a cognitive eval on you?" she asked.

"Ummm, no," I said.

"This is outrageous. Derryen. We are going to get you better. I am going to make sure of it."

At the end of our conversation, I was in both shock and awe. For the first time in almost a year I felt a small glimmer of hope. Just the fact that she had asked about other tests or evaluations that hadn't been conducted made me feel like there was still more that could be done, and maybe something that could still be found. Donna made a long list of tests and treatments that should have been provided but weren't. Even though she was contracted by Workers' Comp, her job was to advocate for me to get the treatments she thought were necessary.

From that first moment, I knew that Donna was going to be my fairy godmother. I knew she would move mountains for me and never let anyone get away with mistreating or neglecting me. And I was right. She was 100 percent dedicated to the people she represented. If I was having trouble getting an appointment, she'd call the doctor's office every day until the issue was resolved. She was present at my first appointment with my new treatment physician, ready to develop a game plan. She called and booked appointments with several doctors and therapists. She was determined that I get the help I needed.

At last, someone believed me—and believed I could get better. And I believed in her, too.

NO STONE UNTURNED

Before Donna, I didn't know what to do besides visiting the ER and going to PT appointments, but it turned out there was more I could do—a *lot* more. If I thought I had been working hard at recovery before, I was in for a surprise. Soon, I was going to as many as nine appointments a week.

First, Donna recommended a new primary doctor who specialized in rehabilitation. Donna consulted with him directly in developing a treatment plan for me. The first test that was ordered was a cognitive evaluation to determine which areas of my brain had been damaged by the multiple blows. This evaluation was no small ask.

The cognitive therapist gave me a six-hour battery of tests in a variety of subjects and formats. The academic geek in me loved it; I thought the problem-solving, pattern matching, word association, and drawing exercises were so cool. Although I was deeply fascinated by the testing, I wasn't sure I was ready to hear the results. Did I want the validation that some areas of my brain had been damaged, and risk losing the one thing that always made me feel unique—my intelligence? Or, would I rather the doctor find nothing, keeping my intelligence intact, but then feeling disappointed in another dead-end test saying there was "nothing wrong with me"? It was a double-edged sword.

After a week of anticipation, my tests had been scored and my results determined. A few of the tests administered provided a baseline rating that would provide an expected result when testing different facets of my cognitive functions. When it came to the areas of simple and complex attention, cognitive flexibility, and working memory, there were noticeable deficits. It was pretty devastating to hear that something I valued so highly was damaged so significantly, and I didn't know if I would be able to repair any of that damage. But at least it was a result.

The cognitive therapist, Maureen, was also a PhD-level neuropsychologist and trauma therapist, and Donna suggested doing trauma therapy with her, too. I liked Maureen, but I wasn't immediately on board. I had told my story fifty million times by then, to dozens of different doctors. It was like reading the same script over and over again. It was just what is was; there were no feelings attached to it. There never were, really. It was just another day in the office and an inmate got the upper hand on me. You win some, you lose some.

Therapy seemed unnecessary, but I was willing to try anything Donna recommended. On the very first day of therapy, I repeated the same script as I had done so many times before and answered her initial follow-up questions.

"Out of curiosity," she said, reaching for a big, blue volume on her bookshelf.

I saw "DSM-V" stamped in big white letters on the cover, and I knew exactly which chapter she was going to. My body tensed up. I recognized this book; I'd consulted it as an undergraduate. It was the Diagnostic and Statistical Manual, compiled by the American Psychiatric Association, a brick of a book filled to the brim with detailed symptom lists used to diagnose mental illnesses.

Mental illnesses? *That isn't me*, I thought; I was only at this session because it was one of the dozens of rehabilitation appointments on my calendar for the month. I was just checking off the boxes, doing what Donna recommended.

Sure enough, Maureen pointed to the section on Post-Traumatic Stress Disorder in the DSM, as follows:

PTSD DIAGNOSTIC CRITERIA

You were exposed to one or more event(s) that involved death or threatened death, actual or threatened serious injury, or threatened sexual violation.

You experience at least one of the following intrusive symptoms associated with the traumatic event:

- Unexpected or expected reoccurring, involuntary, and intrusive upsetting memories of the traumatic event
- Repeated upsetting dreams where the content of the dreams is related to the traumatic event
- The experience of some type of dissociation (for example, flashbacks) where you feel as though the traumatic event is happening again
- Strong and persistent distress upon exposure to cues that are either inside or outside of your body that is connected to your traumatic event
- Strong bodily reactions (for example, increased heart rate) upon exposure to a reminder of the traumatic event
- Frequent avoidance of reminders associated with the traumatic event, as demonstrated by one of the following:
  - Avoidance of thoughts, feelings, or physical sensations that bring up memories of the traumatic event
  - Avoidance of people, places, conversations, activities, objects, or situations that bring up memories of the traumatic event
- At least two of the following negative changes in thoughts and mood that occurred or worsened following the experience of the traumatic event:
  - The inability to remember an important aspect of the traumatic event
  - Persistent and elevated negative evaluations about yourself, others, or the world (for example, "I am unlovable," or "The world is an evil place")
  - Elevated self-blame or blame of others about the cause or consequence of a traumatic event

- A negative emotional state (for example, shame, anger, or fear) that is pervasive
- Loss of interest in activities that you used to enjoy
- Feeling detached from others
- The inability to experience positive emotions (for example, happiness, love, joy)
- At least two of the following changes in arousal that started or worsened following the experience of a traumatic event:
  - Irritability or aggressive behavior
  - Impulsive or self-destructive behavior
  - Feeling constantly "on guard" or like danger is lurking around every corner (or hypervigilance)
  - Heightened startle response
  - Difficulty concentrating
  - Problems sleeping

The above symptoms last for more than one month.

As she read the criteria, I clenched my jaw and held my breath, keeping my negative feelings to myself. *I don't have PTSD*, I thought. *That is not me.* PTSD seemed a bit extreme to me. I was tough enough. The assault wasn't a big deal. I just needed to figure out how to get rid of these migraines.

Even though I admitted that I checked more than enough boxes for each of the criteria, I had an answer for all of them. "I've always had nightmares," I'd tell her. "I'm irritable and emotional because of my head injury," I'd insist. "Everything has to do with my migraines. If only I didn't have this constant pain, I'd be fine," I'd say.

Most importantly, I didn't want to be labeled. I didn't want the label of PTSD to follow me. I still had my eye on eventually getting into a three-letter agency, so I couldn't have a significant mental diagnosis of PTSD associated with my name.

"That's quite all right, Derryen," Maureen said. "I'm not one of those providers driven to place labels on my patients. I just wanted to bring it to your attention for something to consider."

Her words put me at ease. Even though this discussion was happening fifteen months after my assault, I was convinced that the assault had zero effect on me mentally—and she wasn't going to convince me otherwise.

I am tough. I was conditioned for this. I can handle it.

PUSHING THE LIMITS

In addition to the exhaustion that came from waking from nightmares at all hours, and the daily migraines, I juggled two jobs, graduate school, and multiple rehabilitation appointments every day. Donna had me in physical therapy, occupational therapy, cognitive therapy, and cranial-sacral therapy, which usually resulted in two rehab appointments a day. I was pushing my body to the limit.

I was convinced that the harder I worked at my recovery,

the more progress I would make. As an athlete, whenever I sustained an injury, I'd follow rehab and the injury would improve. I was also driven to do whatever I could to enhance my recovery process, because I didn't like not working. I didn't like being dependent on others. I didn't want to lose my independence.

So, I did what I do best—work myself to exhaustion so I wouldn't have to deal with anything else. Unfortunately, brain injuries are not like other physical injuries, and I learned that the hard way.

One night, I went out to dinner with a friend. I suddenly had this terrible feeling come over me. It was nothing I had ever felt before, and I thought I was going to be sick. I didn't want to make a scene, so I got up from the table and tried to walk casually to the bathroom. Halfway across the restaurant, my body weakened and everything started to go dark. I tried to grab onto a half wall for support.

I lost consciousness and fell to the floor.

Nobody even noticed I collapsed. I was still on the floor when I regained consciousness. My body was completely paralyzed, but I could hear everything that was going on around me. "Oh my god, are you okay?" someone said, finally noticing me on the ground. "Oh my god, I didn't even see her," another remarked. They sat me on a barstool and started asking me questions. "Do you have epilepsy? Are you having a seizure?"

I understood them perfectly but was unable to answer them. I couldn't speak and could barely move. I was only able to shake my head.

"Are you drunk? How much have you had to drink?" I was terrified they were going to throw me out of the restaurant for thinking I was intoxicated when I wasn't, and that I was going to freeze to death on the sidewalk.

"Should we call an ambulance?" I wanted to yell, "No!" and get out of there as fast as I could.

So much for not making a scene, but in that moment, something shifted. It finally clicked for me: I'd been pushing my body way too hard, and it finally reached its breaking point. I'd been so obsessed with trying to get better that I was actually making my condition worse. This wasn't something I could will away with hard work. The harder I fought, the harder it fought me back.

My rehabilitation doctors were absolutely incredible. When one of them noticed this medical episode in my file, she called me immediately to check in and express her concern. Each of my doctors had told me that I was working too hard and needed to cut back, but I brushed it off. I had been going at this pace for over a year and a half. Well, it finally caught up with me.

I had to take better care of myself.

VISION LOSS

Each of my providers were dedicated to using their specific skillset to try to provide me with some answers or improvement in one region of my functioning or another. During one of my visits with my occupational therapist, I told her about my vision.

"I'm struggling with depth perception on my right side, especially while driving," I told her. She recommended I undergo a visual field test, which measures an individual's entire scope of vision and detects areas of vision loss.

This test provided me with the first significant finding since the assault, nearly eighteen months later. The results of the test were represented in a map of both eyes, with vision loss represented as patterned squares in the areas of deficit. The evaluation of my left eye came back perfect—not a single patterned square to be found. My right eye, however, counted eleven areas of deficit. This was permanent vision loss.

But this test only scratched the surface.

After this discovery, I was determined to leave no stone unturned, medically speaking, even when I was so sick of doctors and their judgmental attitudes. I continued to wonder what else was left to be found. It had been a year and a half since the assault, and I felt like I was just starting to get some answers.

NEURO-OPTOMETRY

Donna's next assignment for me was to visit a neuro-optometrist. Neuro-optometrists treat individuals who have vision problems associated with neurological disease, trauma, metabolic, or congenital conditions. When I met the neuro-optometrist, a professional designation I didn't even know existed, his first comment made me want to walk out of his office.

"Wow, Derryen. Your file is pretty thick. You've seen a lot of doctors."

Oh, great; another doctor who's gonna question me, I thought. *He probably thinks I'm a hypochondriac or a pain-med junkie.*

I bit my tongue and didn't walk out—and I'm glad I stayed. He conducted tests I had never seen before. He checked how fast my pupils dilated and constricted. He had me hold a stick with a rounded top in my outstretched hands and asked me to bring it toward my center until I thought it was directly in front of my nose.

Then I donned some strange goggles with exchangeable lenses and walked up and down the hallway. He asked me what I felt. It was the most bizarre feeling. For some reason, wearing the strange goggles altered something in me physically.

"I feel like I'm walking upright," I reported. "I feel like my body has been slouched to the right until now."

Bingo.

"You have something called Visual Midline Shift Syndrome."

Visual Midline Shift Syndrome is a mismatch between visual and spatial information processed by the brain. Because of brain changes brought on by my assault, my sensory feedback loop was out of whack. The spot I saw as center, right in front of my nose, was actually an inch off to the side. That explained why I couldn't walk down the stairs without hanging on for dear life—nothing was where I thought it was. It also explained why driving was such a terrifying experience—looking at anything at a distance skewed my visual center even more, so I couldn't orient where other cars were. And no wonder it was so draining to take a walk in the woods; as I stepped over tree roots and ducked under branches, my brain was working overtime recalibrating my position in space with each step.

Is this behind my intense migraines? Did we just find the holy grail of why my head hurts so bad? I was so hopeful that this was the answer to all my problems. Finally!

But this wasn't his only finding. The neuro-optometrist also checked my eyes the same way dozens of doctors had done before, but he noticed something different. He told me that a normal pupil takes ten to fifteen seconds to dilate after it is exposed to light. My pupils were dilating in two to three seconds. This meant that my sympathetic nervous system was operating at a rate of five times what is should be; it was in overdrive. My body was in constant "fight or flight" even when I was just doing my normal daily tasks.

This was not only an indicator that my brain was having difficulty processing stimuli; it was also a physiological indicator of PTSD (but that still wasn't enough evidence for me to accept the diagnosis).

Miracle of miracles, there was a treatment for Visual Midline Shift Syndrome—special prismatic glasses that would help me recalibrate my visual processing system. The process was said to take about a year to correct, but that was a small price to pay for a validated treatment. It was mindblowing to wear them, because not only did they let me see the world correctly for the first time in a year and a half, but they showed me how literally off-center my vision had been all this time. When I pulled the glasses down my nose and peered over them, there was a clear distinction between where the object was supposed to be and where it appeared to me. When I pushed the glasses back up, the world snapped back into square. Sweet relief.

This is it, I thought. *This is going to cure my migraines!*

As the months went by, wearing the glasses changed the way my brain processed visual input, and that shift became smaller and smaller, until I didn't need them anymore. Instead of taking a year, it only took four months.

I could move around the world normally at last.

NO RELIEF

Unfortunately, even though I could stand up straight, navigate a hallway, drive a car, and go on hikes, I still had excruciating migraines. None of the treatments so far had relieved them.

Well, what's next? Is there anything left to uncover? With each discovery, hope flooded my psyche that we finally found the cause of my pain, only to be met with disappointment when the treatment, despite its success, didn't actually get the pain to go away. The roller coaster of highs and lows left me emotionally exhausted.

I was ready to quit. *Maybe this is my new normal,* I told myself. *Maybe I just have to accept it and deal with it.*

Thank goodness for Donna. She refused to give up.

ALTERNATIVE METHODS

Since we exhausted all conventional migraine treatments, Donna started to look into alternative methods. She and my neuropsychologist, Maureen, listened to a presentation given by a migraine surgeon that they thought could potentially benefit me. Together, they vetted him thoroughly and agreed that this was the next best step for me.

Prior to my initial consultation, I filled out a twelve-page questionnaire with some surprising questions on it. I thought I had heard *all* the questions about migraines at that point, but I guess not—which gave me some hope. Doctors and nurses frequently asked what made my migraines better and what made them worse. My answer was always the same: nothing. From the time I got up in the morning until the time I went to bed, it was the same. There was no better.

Nobody believed me, but here on the page there was a new question: Is the pain constant, without fluctuation?

What? That's a legitimate thing? Because the answer was yes. *Maybe I'm not crazy. Maybe there is something that explains what I have been experiencing, and maybe he knows what it is!* Maybe this doctor was different.

And he was. He asked very specific questions about pain, pressure, and lighting sensations. He listened when I told him the pain originated at the back of my neck. He felt different nerves around my head and asked me questions about any sensations I felt. He explained that migraines usually happen in one of three places—the temporal region, right behind the temples; in between the eyes; or in the occipital region, at the back of the neck.

Really? The back of the neck? Why am I just hearing this now? This is exactly what I had been complaining about for almost two years. But my symptoms didn't mean anything to anyone else.

The medical diagnosis I was given: occipital neuralgia. There were two different treatments on the table. Botox and surgery. I opted for the Botox first to gauge if my situation actually warranted surgery, or if it could be mitigated with two injections to the back of my skull every three months.

Even better, the doctor administered the shot right then and there, and I was completely shocked by the results.

The first three weeks after the Botox injections were unbelievable. For the first time in nearly two years, I felt like I had woken up out of a fog. My migraines had been severely reduced. I felt genuine happiness like I hadn't experienced in a long time. It was truly euphoric.

We did it! We finally found the solution! I can live again!

Unfortunately, this was just another short-lived improvement, as the Botox wore off after only three weeks, instead of three months. My debilitating migraines returned. Botox can't be administered again until after that three-month mark has passed, so I couldn't go back and get another set of shots. I only had one option left on the table—and if surgery could fix this, I was in.

Or was I? Nothing is ever simple in medicine, and the recommended surgery was a lot for me to take in. The doctor explained that the standard operation to treat migraines involved treating nerves in all three suspect locations at the same time. Thus, he would make several incisions, including one that would go from ear to ear along the back of my head, one in front of each ear, and another above each eyelid. And they would have to shave some of my hair.

Oh God, I thought, *not my hair!*

I know how that sounds—incredibly vain and entirely

beside the point—but my sense of identity was so fragile at the time, I couldn't stand the idea of being disfigured. I was exhausted and emotionally drained from the never-ending roller-coaster ride of hope and despair.

With Donna's help, I had engaged in every rehabilitation therapy possible for nearly two years, and nothing helped the migraines. Surgery was my last option. I had no choice but to take it.

After consulting with my surgeon on my follow-up visit, we agreed that only treating my occipital region seemed the most reasonable, as my symptoms were primarily the result of an injury and not from genetic susceptibility to migraines. He would make an incision—but only one—and decompress the four nerves in the back of my head. This meant examining the nerves to make sure no muscles or blood vessels were pressing up against them, as well as reworking the surrounding structures to ensure that nothing impinged on the nerves.

The doctor really sold it, telling me that surgery in this area had the easiest recovery period—and that he would shave as little of my hair as possible—but he also shared the risks. Based on his examination, he thought he might have to remove several nerves, but he wouldn't know until he got in there and could see the physical structures. After surgery, my head would feel numb. He told me that it would take up to a couple of months for me to regain feeling in the back of my head. If they did remove a nerve, I would permanently lose feeling in a region of my scalp.

I wondered if it was worth it; removing a nerve sounded so drastic. Was I just trading arsenic for cyanide? The surgeon assured me there was no risk of motor function damage, because these were sensory nerves. The procedure itself wasn't especially invasive, as they were only going through a few layers of skin to get to the nerves. Finally, he told me the biggest risk was probably infection if I didn't follow after-care instructions, and I was nothing if not the poster child for compliance.

I knew I had to do it. It was the most specifically targeted intervention I'd heard of, and it addressed the region I had been complaining about for almost two years. There was obviously something going on there. I just had to put trust in the specialist that there would be a positive outcome.

Once I decided, I wanted it done right away, but getting the surgery booked was an incredible hassle. After a month of trying to sort it out myself, I called Donna. Thank God for her help; she was able to get answers out of Workers' Compensation and the doctor's scheduling secretary that no number of calls from me could achieve. She got me a surgery date in June, and I started counting down the days.

It was set for a Thursday. I was anxious the entire week prior. I carefully organized all my cases from work since I was going to be out for a few weeks. I had requested the time off from both jobs; everything was set. The Monday before my surgery, I received an email from the hospital: "Your surgery has been rescheduled for mid-July."

They couldn't even call me to reschedule? They sent me an email? And I have to bear this pain for five more weeks? It's not fair! It's not fair!

I was devastated. I threw my phone down the hallway and collapsed on the floor, bawling.

Was this a sign? I wondered. Maybe surgery was a bad idea. Maybe I shouldn't go through with this after all. I was losing faith in the process and didn't have the confidence that I had during the last consultation. Thank goodness for my mom, who came to my rescue. She comforted me in my misery and made me feel confident in my decision.

When doctors suggested medication to help me manage the pain for the next five weeks, I agreed. I'd always been adamantly anti-medication and didn't take anything up until this point. Just thinking about dealing with the pain for another five weeks was unbearable. At this point, I was willing to take anything to help. The medication the doctor prescribed was specifically for nerve pain, but it also had a mood-boosting component to it. I had little faith that a pill could help regulate my crazy emotions, but after taking it for a few days, to my delight, it did.

I started counting down the days to my surgery. Again.

THE DAY FINALLY ARRIVED

Five weeks passed and my second surgery date arrived. I was so nervous. I couldn't help but think something else was going to go wrong. In fact, we got off to a rough start. My father drove me two hours to the hospital, and I got there at 6:45 a.m. to do all the paperwork, meet the anesthesiologist, and get prepped for a 7:30 a.m. surgery. At 7:30 the nursing staff told me they were ready to go; they were just waiting on the surgeon.

At 8 a.m. there was still no sign of him. I was freaking out, and my dad was furious. I thought they were going to cancel my surgery for the second time on me. By 8:15, the nurse returned to say they had called him and he was on his way.

On his way. Incredible. My nerves were through the roof, and I felt like throwing up. The anticipation was killing me. When he finally arrived at 8:30, he didn't even apologize.

My dad, who is usually very confrontational, looked him calmly in the eye and said, "Are you up for this?"

The doctor said, "Yeah, why do you ask?"

"Because you're an hour late." I know how much restraint it took for him to stop at that, but he knew we wanted to stay on this guy's good side, as he was the one who would be cutting me open. The nursing staff wheeled me back into the operating room, complaining all the while about the late start and how none of them were informed. Now they were trying to locate the anesthesiologist who left to attend to other patients with surgeries scheduled for 8:30.

Everything was going wrong. It felt like I made the wrong decision. I did my best to hold it together, but inside I wanted to explode and go home.

While the surgical nurses were getting everything situated, I started feeling a burning pain in my hand with the IV. It caught me off guard, and I started screaming, "Ow, ow, ow!" The pain was enough to break down what I was trying to hold together. Tears streamed down my face and I couldn't control them. I was utterly terrified.

The surgical nurse immediately responded by checking with another nurse to make sure they hadn't started administering anything through my IV. She rubbed my hand to make it feel better, wiped away my tears, and rubbed my cheek. I was so overwhelmed, and her gesture comforted me greatly and put me at ease. That small human gesture made all the difference. I wish I knew who she was so I could tell her how much that meant to me.

The anesthesiologist arrived, I counted down from ten, not even making it to six when the lights went out.

WAKING UP

Three and a half hours later, the surgery was done. It took several nurses to wake me up from the anesthesia.

"Derryen, you've got to open your eyes," they urged, but I didn't want to. I just wanted to sleep. I could have slept all day, but they were waving alcohol wipes under my nose to spark some life into me. I felt nauseous, but couldn't feel much of anything else.

The surgeon came in and explained what he found. "We decompressed three nerves, but the fourth one was quite a surprise. When we went in, we saw that you had a muscle completely branched around one of your lesser occipital nerves, severely constricting it." He mentioned that some of the doctors in the operating room had never seen something like that before.

"I removed the nerve and cut some muscles to make more space," he continued.

That was it! The holy grail! We finally found it! It was what had been causing my migraines this whole time.

A wave of emotion washed over me. I felt so vindicated. There *was* something physically wrong—in the area I was experiencing physical pain. To every doctor who mistreated me, judged my situation, or thought I was making it up or that it was all in my head: you were wrong! I'd known all along that's where the pain was coming from.

A nurse handed me some ointment and some pain meds, got me dressed, and helped my dad walk me to the car, where I planned to sleep some more. As soon as I sat down in the front seat, however, the anesthesia must have worn off completely because I felt alert and awake. For the first time in a long time, I felt fine. Really fine. The nausea was gone, and I wasn't in any pain.

I was ready for a relaxing, scenic ride home. Everything was going to be just fine.

Or was it?

CHAPTER SIX

||||||||||||||||||||

POST-SURGERY IDENTITY

Recovery was a bumpy ride.

For the first few days post-surgery, I felt like Frankenstein with a massive suture in the back of my head. Because they cut muscles, I couldn't move my head in any direction, and the entire back of my head felt numb and tight at the same time, which was unsettling. My neck muscles were so stiff that I had to sleep flat on my back, when I'm usually an all-night thrasher. Needless to say, I didn't get much sleep. And when it came time to pick my head up off the pillow in the morning, I simply couldn't do it. I needed someone to lift it for me. I was also expected to apply cream to the eight-inch incision multiple times a day to prevent infection. I needed to rely on someone else for that, too. I had always prided myself on being independent and self-sufficient, so being reliant on others was a huge shift for me.

My boyfriend did everything for me after the surgery. He kept track of my medications and put the ointment on my incision. He counted the hours between prescribed treatments, reminded me when I was supposed to apply ice, and wrestled the ice pack away from me after the prescribed twenty minutes, because it felt so good that I didn't want to give it up. If I stood in the shower in tears, he'd come and wash my hair. Simple things like that were incredibly important to me, because I'd felt ugly and dehumanized for so long, and here was someone who still cared for me.

When the numbness began to subside, I expected the pressure in my head to return, but to my astonishment and delight, it didn't. It was gone. By three weeks out, the migraines were better, too. I couldn't believe it. It was a freaking miracle. I was so excited I was all but jumping up and down when I told my primary-care doctor how well I was doing, but he was cautious, clearly worried I was being overly optimistic. I wasn't worried, though; I knew something big had changed—and I've been mostly migraine-free since then. I do have occasional phantom pains in the nerve that's no longer there, but they last a couple of minutes and then go away.

I was beyond thankful to wake up each morning without

pain. What a relief! I felt optimistic about my future for the first time in years. My natural drive and motivation returned. Without the constant distraction of the pressure in my head, I felt mentally sharper, which made my job much easier. I had more energy and put it to use making spreadsheets, organizing my cases, and getting new systems in place. Coworkers commented that I was glowing and seemed to have more life in me. Two days after I got my stitches out, I even took my two-year competency test for a promotion and passed the first time.

The pending promotion should have felt like a major victory, but even as the circumstances of my life turned a corner, something inside shifted to a dark place; I didn't feel the excitement I thought I should be feeling. In fact, I felt oddly disconnected from my successes. All I felt was an intense grief and sadness that felt completely out of place. It was as if I was going through a breakup, or as if someone close to me had died. I couldn't make any sense of it.

I so badly wanted to be fully recovered, to say I felt like my old self again, but I couldn't, because I wasn't my old self at all. I was no longer the injured person who couldn't deal with life because of the debilitating pain, but I also wasn't the person who wanted to profile serial killers and track down bad guys. I was no longer attracted to crime topics—real or on TV. After all the horror I had seen in real life, I had no interest in seeing fictional horrors. And I definitely wasn't the girl who thought she could control her world by following the rules; that clearly had not worked.

So, who was I?

UNCOVERING MY NEW IDENTITY

Was I someone who would now be prone to massive mood swings? It seemed like it—my emotions were so extreme, ranging from intense anger to bottomless sorrow, and I couldn't explain why.

On the surface, everything in my life was going incredibly well. My surgery and recovery couldn't have gone better (no infections!). I was a superstar at work. I bought a beautiful house the year prior. I completed my master's degree five months after surgery. I could support myself, I had food to eat and clothes to wear, and I didn't wake up in horrendous pain every day. So, why the hell was I upset all the time?

I couldn't tie these feelings to anything tangible, which was incredibly frustrating. There was nothing in my life that was making me unhappy. There was nothing for me to fix. It was just this innate pain that I couldn't shake. And I was afraid to tell anyone, frankly, because if anyone knew how chaotic and intense my feelings were, they would surely shuffle me off to the psych ward.

I went on crying jags seemingly out of the blue. I no longer suffered from migraines, but I still felt awful. I couldn't figure out how to tell anyone that I was consumed by darkness every second of every day. Or how I hadn't been sleeping because I still had nightmares (more on this in a moment). Or how I had three more double shifts to work in the next three days and I didn't know how I was going to do it. I just cried.

My boyfriend at the time tried to help. "Don't cry," he'd tell me. "Why are you crying? There's nothing to cry about." That made me cry even harder. He was right—there wasn't anything to cry about. My life *was* better! He got frustrated with me and distanced himself, because he just didn't understand. How could he? He'd never been through anything like this, and I wasn't explaining myself at all. But I simply couldn't find the words.

I did try, though. I knew when I was being irrational, and I would tell him I was just having a rough day. The best I could do was to explain that my mood swings weren't logical, but they were intense and out of my control. "You'll recover," he reassured me. "Life is good. I don't understand why you're upset."

I wasn't just upset; I was clinically depressed, but unless you've gone through that, you don't understand what it's like. I had no idea how debilitating depression could be until it happened to me, so I couldn't expect him to understand. I used to be one of those people who thought the answer to depression was taking better care of yourself, and all of those negative feelings would magically go away. Needless to say, after experiencing the sheer magnitude of severe depression, my perspective changed.

If someone is in crutches or in a cast, people can visually see that they are physically injured. They automatically know they will struggle with various daily life activities; they will struggle simply trying to take care of themselves. The various associative traumas that stem from head injuries, on the other hand, are not visible. You can't see depression, or sadness, or grief. When someone looked at me, they didn't see any injuries, so they'd assume I was okay, or normal. In reality, I was suffering from an invisible injury. No one could see that I woke up exhausted and drained every day. No one could see the frustration I felt internally about losing control over my emotions. No one could see how I was triggered by something that shouldn't have been a big deal. Because they couldn't visibly see my injury, they didn't understand why I reacted the way I did. And because they didn't understand, I started to hide my true feelings. I put a lot of pressure on myself to try to appear a certain way, which only made things worse.

Then one day, I sent my boyfriend a cartoon* called "How to Take Care of a Sad Person" to try to shed some light on my feelings and how he could help me, even if he didn't understand.

HOW TO TAKE CARE OF A SAD PERSON

1. Lay out a blanket.
2. Put the sad person in the blanket.
3. Roll them up like a sushi roll.
4. Sit sushi roll on the couch.
5. Hug sushi roll close.
6. Put on sushi roll's favorite TV show.
7. Bring sushi roll a snack.

A few days later, I was a miserable mess, all pent up and angry, sitting on the couch fuming. My boyfriend was puttering around the house when he came back with a blanket. Without saying a word, he spread it out on the giant ottoman, picked me up and put me in it, wrapped me up, and sat me back down on the couch. That kind, thoughtful gesture didn't stop my crying—in fact it kicked it up a notch—but now I was crying because he was making an effort to comfort me in the way I needed to be comforted.

With his acceptance, I slowly started spitting out words to describe my inner landscape, to try to give him some idea of how I was feeling. "I'm just frustrated," I'd say. "I'm over-

---

* https://www.boredpanda.com/how-to-care-for-little-sad-person-john-saddington/?utm_source=google&utm_medium=organic&utm_campaign=organic

whelmed." That didn't begin to communicate the intense feelings of grief and loss I was experiencing, but it was a start. I *was* overwhelmed by these feelings; they seemed so out of proportion to anything going on in my life, and they were so out of control. They became so dark and intense that I started to question my purpose in life.

Is life even worth living like this?

NOTHING LEFT TO GIVE

For the nine months prior to my surgery, I'd always looked forward to working through my trauma at my weekly therapy sessions with Maureen, but suddenly, I didn't want to go anymore. I didn't want to talk to anyone. I didn't want to be around anyone. I felt ugly and just wanted to be left alone, so I canceled my therapy session that week. "Hey, Maureen," I texted. "I don't want to meet this week."

I didn't want to sit across from her and talk. She would see that there was something I wasn't telling her, and I just didn't want to go there until I could get a better handle on things by myself. "Okay, then," she texted back right away. "How about we go for a walk and get some ice cream?"

That Maureen is one wise woman. She bribed me into going to therapy, and I'm grateful she did. My feelings were so strong, I could barely look at her when I spoke. By walking along by her side, I didn't have to register her gaze while I talked about how heavy and lost I felt, how ashamed and embarrassed I was by my mood swings, and how I was losing my will to live and I couldn't figure out why.

"I'm in so much emotional pain," I said, "but I don't have any explanation for it. I have nowhere to put it. And it's so real and heavy, driving me to such depths of sadness, I don't know what to do. I don't want to die, but I don't want to live like this, either. I don't have any fight left in me. I don't have anything left to give."

If I expected my confession to horrify her, I couldn't have been more wrong.

"Honestly," said Maureen, "I'd be more concerned if you weren't experiencing these feelings. You've been through the wringer." When I heard her words, I felt like I could finally exhale after holding my breath too long. I had been so scared to say anything about my crazy emotions, but here she was validating them. They were normal. Oh, how I needed to hear those words.

Shortly after our session, I continued my search for answers about what I was going through. I stumbled on an article in a medical journal that made me feel even more validated. It was about a condition called "post-operative depression," which can happen after surgery because the unconscious part of you realizes how vulnerable you were on that operating table, even if you didn't acknowledge it consciously. As far as your body is concerned, you have just been attacked, so it withdraws through depressive symptoms. The symptoms tend to be worse if the procedure involves removing something from the body or results in physical limitations afterward. And it's even worse if the surgery reawakens old trauma—which it absolutely did. It definitely flared up the emotional aspect from my assault that I still hadn't fully dealt with yet.

This made sense to me, and boy, did I relate to it all. It was such a relief. I wasn't going crazy after all. This was something others have also experienced post-surgery. It was normal.

And the best news was that it would get better.

EXHAUSTING NIGHTMARES AND PTSD

Despite finding the holy-grail answer to my migraines and getting the surgery to treat them, I still experienced horribly violent dreams—dreams where I got stabbed, tortured, chased, and beaten. I had one where I got shot five times in the face and felt every single bullet pierce my body. The dreams came in waves (they still do), and they feel very, very real. When I wake up from one of these "bad dreams," I'm utterly exhausted, as if I finished running a marathon.

The exhaustion became so severe that it was affecting my quality of life. I would wake up drained with zero energy, and yet I had to go into work for a double shift. I've always worked a lot, and I've always been tired, but this was different. I reached a hellish level of exhaustion where I just couldn't do it anymore.

This is not normal, I thought to myself. *I shouldn't be this debilitated.*

Before the surgery, I blamed the nightmares and subsequent exhaustion on my migraines. *If only I didn't have these migraines, I would be okay.* I thought I did everything I could: the processing, the therapy, the months and months of recovery, yet here I was still dealing with these night terrors. Except this time, I had no excuse. I didn't have an explanation for why they continued.

Clearly, there was something that I wasn't acknowledging.

I thought back to my first therapy session with Maureen where she brought up PTSD. Perhaps she was right. The logical part of me knew I met the criteria, even back then. But I didn't want to accept it. I wasn't emotionally ready to accept it.

Nine months of therapy and a surgery later, I still checked off a lot of the boxes under PSTD's criteria. That explained the nightmares, the sleeping problems, and the exhaustion. That explained the inability to experience positive emotions surrounding my successes (promotion at work, buying a house, etc.). That explained my disinterest in anything relating to crime (on TV or in the real world). Maybe I did suffer from PTSD.

Gradually, the emotional side of me finally joined the logical part: Maureen was right all along.

And of course she was right; she's trained in head injuries and trauma! But I couldn't see that at the time; I was still in survival mode. At my next therapy session with Maureen, I came in defeated. "I thought that I had already worked through everything that I needed to work through," I confessed. "I thought my surgery was the holy grail to all my problems."

"This is all a part of your healing journey, Derryen," Maureen said. "As time goes on and things change, there will be new grief to process—and we'll work through it."

I still felt agitated, upset, and depressed—emotions I associated with the pain from the migraines. I thought once the pain was addressed, it would address these feelings, too. But I was wrong. Maureen reminded me that I simply ended one chapter and started another. Even after processing my feelings with Maureen for nine months in therapy, she told me that they'd come back in new ways—especially as I figured out what my new identity was—leaving me with new grief to process.

My work was far from over. In fact, it was just beginning. I continued to meet with Maureen on a weekly basis to process through these feelings and reorient my life to my new normal.

I knew the plan I created for myself when I was a little girl was no longer a reality. I said goodbye to ever working for a federal agency. Not only did I come out as a different person through this whole ordeal; I confided that I had suicidal thoughts to my therapist, so there was a record of that. No three-letter agency would accept me now, anyway.

EMOTIONAL ROLLER COASTER

It took nine months of therapy and a surgery for me to finally admit to myself that I was suffering from PTSD, but looking back now, I started experiencing emotional shifts long before the assault took place.

Before I started working at the jail, I watched every serial-killer documentary and jail reality show and usually fell asleep to horror movies—which had always been my favorite. Shortly after I started working at the jail, however, I no longer watched movies or shows that involved violence or criminals. The things I could never get enough of suddenly began to disturb me, even early into my time working at the jail. When you watch documentaries about serial killers and see their pictures, you might think to yourself, "Wow, that guy looks so evil." But working at the jail taught me that evil doesn't have a look. Some juveniles came from great families. Many were highly intelligent individuals who conducted themselves like model citizens. They appeared clean-cut, and many seemed unthreatening. And yet, they were convicted of some of the most heinous crimes you can imagine.

After a few months at the jail, I couldn't talk about things that were on the local news. "Did you see the story about the woman who was found in the woods?" my mom would ask. "Did you read about the child who went missing?"

"No," I would respond coldly. "I don't care to know about it." Looking back now, I can see that this was early onset of PTSD.

Every day at work, I witnessed inmates assault each other. Every day, I listened to inmates threaten my life, the lives of my coworkers, and the lives of their fellow inmates. I witnessed inmates try to take their own life on more occasions than I care to count—and I was the first responder to an inmate who had successfully done so. I listened as inmates confided in me about the horrific abuses they were subjected to in their lives. I did all of that for nearly two years, and I later learned that it's a weight you can't leave at the door when you clock out of work, despite your best efforts.

Afterward, I just didn't have any more room for bleak narratives. I couldn't bear to hear anything I didn't have to.

When working in the jail, I compartmentalized incredibly well, and everything I saw or dealt with never bothered me—or at least that's what I told myself. With each horrific thing I witnessed, I grew more and more rigid, internally and mentally building my armor. *I was tough. I could handle this.* This prevailing mentality stuck with me for years. The first time I started to take that armor off was when I started therapy with Maureen, fifteen months after the assault.

That same month, I started the final course to complete my master's degree in criminal justice—a class titled "Victimology." I had registered for this course the year prior, but withdrew after the suicide of that young inmate I had administered CPR to at the jail. I withdrew because I knew focusing on that content so soon after losing an inmate would be very demanding on me mentally (I was still suffering from my intense migraines during this time). I knew my quality of work would have suffered, so I decided to drop the class and wait a year.

When faced with this course the second time, I was ready—

or so I thought. The course required reading a supplemental book entitled *The Ride*, which I started reading before the class started. The book outlined the graphic murder of a child by a pedophile, the investigation, and the aftermath. The pages illustrated the grief experienced by the parents, the personality of the young child, and the cold-blooded nature of the killer. All of this was hitting way too close to home, especially as the one-year anniversary of the inmate's death was also happening at the same time.

Things were compounding and I started breaking down. The last step in achieving my master's degree was going to be the hardest one. For the first time in a year, I grieved the loss of this young individual. My heart wept for him, his pain, and that he would never experience the joy and happiness that life has to offer.

The more time that passed working in a "normal" work environment, the more I became sensitized to the chaos and the horrors I had seen. I witnessed inmates getting jumped and arms getting broken; I witnessed kids trying to infect staff with communicable diseases by spitting blood at them; and I witnessed several inmates try to take their own lives. Every day was a new horror. I always considered those events to be "just another day in the office," and at the time, I didn't mind the chaos. I looked at them as opportunities for me to prove myself, and I never shied away from the chance at doing so. It never bothered me in the moment, but the longer I spent outside of that environment, the more those memories started to haunt me.

With the help of Maureen, I finally started processing all the grief that I buried and compartmentalized for so long. It took nine months of therapy to admit that I wasn't "fine" after the assault—which happened fifteen months before therapy. So, in total, it took me two years to get to a place of acceptance of what actually happened to me. Two years! It was a lot of work, and at times it was incredibly uncomfortable and unpleasant.

But I did it.

A LONG AND WINDING ROAD

Someone once told me that traumatic events are as significant as physical injuries. If you broke a bone in your leg, you wouldn't leave it to heal on its own. It is the same with traumatic events; you can't leave your mind to heal on its own. You need to take the necessary steps to repair the damage—which may take years and a variety of forms.

Trying to regain a normal life after my surgery while navigating the waters of PTSD was rough. In an effort to help control my wildly varying emotions, I eventually agreed to increase the dose of the nerve pain medication I was taking, which had mood-boosting effects. Although this helped, I felt like every time I took a step forward, I took two steps back.

Despite physically improving and doing well in therapy, my relationship with my boyfriend started to fall apart. I tried to control my emotions and PTSD, to get better, and to be who my boyfriend wanted me to be, but as much as I tried, it wasn't enough. His lack of understanding and subtle criticisms when I was already down on myself didn't help. Our relationship started deteriorating in September, four months after my surgery, and we eventually called it quits a couple of months later.

Breaking up on top of everything else going on obviously didn't help my mental state. I felt ugly, unwanted, and alone. I spiraled out again into a hole of depression. Thank goodness for my mom. "Let's go to the animal shelter," she suggested one particularly blue day.

"No, mom," I told her. "I don't want to."

"Come on, Derryen. If anything, the little kitties will make you smile. It'll be fun!"

"Okay, fine," I said. "Twist my arm."

When we entered the cat area, we saw two adorable little kitten brothers, and I immediately fell in love. *These guys are going home with me*, I told myself. And they did. I named them Kanga and Roo, and they have been hugely helpful in my recovery. Having two cats to care for lifted my spirits in ways I never thought possible. Their unconditional love was (and still is) hugely powerful. While I previously hated sitting at home because being alone made me restless, Kanga and Roo have given me peace in my home and in my mind.

They gave me reason and purpose, and they kept me from feeling alone. I continue to suffer from debilitating night terrors almost every night, which cause me to wake up drenched in sweat. When I am having a night terror, Kanga will come and lie on my chest and lick my face, offering comfort or trying to wake me up from my nightmare. His compassion for me leaves me in awe.

My cats have been more therapeutic than I could have ever imagined, and they have given me more than I could have ever asked for—which goes to show that therapy can come in a variety of forms; you just have to be open-minded and willing to receive.

ACCEPTING HELP

Maybe you're suffering from trauma and aren't getting the help you deserve. If that's the case, I want to encourage you to be brave and ask for help. Seek it out. Be open to it. Accept it.

I know, I know; that's easier said than done. It sure was for me. Before Donna, Maureen, and the countless doctors who have helped me on my journey, I had always done everything myself. I'd even resisted help from friends and family. I didn't want to come across as weak, and I definitely didn't want to feel like a burden to them.

For weeks after the assault, I didn't tell a soul what I was going through. I was in unbearable pain every minute of every day when I lived at my parents' house, but I was careful not to let them see it. I didn't want them to see any vulnerability.

It took me a long time to acknowledge that I couldn't do it all alone and that I needed help from others.

The first time I let the walls come down was when my mentor called to have a local police officer check in on me, and I admitted to my mother how dreadful I felt. For the first time, I conceded that I was in trouble, and I learned an important lesson: requesting aid didn't bring on the end of the world. In fact, it brought me empathy and understanding. As much as I didn't want to go to the hospital that day, I took so much comfort in the mere fact that my mom drove me directly to the ER and sat in that waiting room with me for three hours. She couldn't fix everything, but she could be there for me.

I have gotten better at asking for help, but it didn't come

easily, and I still impose super high expectations of myself. When I planned for my surgery, for example, I didn't ask for the month off I needed to recover. Instead, I told colleagues I would return to work the week that my stitches came out, just two weeks after my surgery.

I've also since learned to speak up for myself. My boyfriend wanted to go camping the weekend after my surgery, but all I really wanted to do was rest. I didn't want to risk an infection, and sleeping would have been unbearably uncomfortable. After agreeing this wasn't the best idea, he wanted to take a road trip instead. I couldn't advocate for myself this time, so instead of asking him to stay home so I could rest just two days after my surgery, I endured a painful five-hour round-trip drive, which only made the muscles in my neck feel worse since I couldn't move my head whatsoever. I know now I should have spoken up for myself and that everyone would have understood that I needed time to lie low, but I just didn't know how to put myself first that way.

Even now, if I ask anyone for anything, I feel like I should make it up to them, even if the help is freely given. After some recent dental surgery, for example, I had to miss a shift at the restaurant, and although nobody blinked an eye, I felt so awful that I picked up an extra shift to make up for my absence.

I'm a work in progress, for sure, but I'm learning. I hated

taking time off from my revenue job for all of my rehab appointments, even though the time was covered by Workers' Comp. I was worried about being less productive and letting everyone down. In reality, my rehab work made me a better employee. When the appointments ended, I returned to work with so much more energy and focus that I was much *more* productive. Plus, I was recovering my cognitive abilities, so I was much more efficient—I no longer had to go over tasks again and again to make sure I'd completed everything I was supposed to. Everything was easier, and the quality of my work was better than ever.

What a surprise—asking for help actually helped. I wouldn't have been able to achieve this level of peace and stability without accepting outside help and being willing to put in the hard work. I know you can find peace, too. But it starts with accepting help.

In reflecting on my journey, I feel inspired to help others—not only those who suffer from trauma, but also those who are helping victims of trauma. Although everyone will experience trauma differently, I want to shed light on how you could help someone on their recovery journey. In the next chapter, I'll share some insight and advice that I hope you will find helpful.

CHAPTER SEVEN

|||||||||||||||||||||||

GIVING HELP

In hindsight, I'm grateful to every single person who tried to help me, even if they didn't know it at the time. I occasionally lashed out at people who tried to assist me on my recovery journey, and I felt incredibly guilty after.

If you're caring for a family member or friend with a head injury, PTSD, or other trauma, you've probably been on the receiving end of one of those lashings. Anger and resistance are common symptoms of a head injury, so try not to take it personally. It's not about you; it's about everything your loved one has been through. Trauma can have a wide range of effects on a person; symptoms can go beyond anger and resistance. In fact, anger and resistance are surface-level emotions, which often stem from deeper issues. Your loved one can be experiencing general emotional dysregulation, denial, confusion, and helplessness. They could be feeling extra vulnerable, or victimized. They could be feeling like they've lost control, which only enhances all of these feelings. Most importantly, your loved one might not be able to make these connections.

So where does that leave you as a caregiver? You probably feel helpless, too. Perhaps you feel powerless, that nothing you do will make a difference. That's not true. Recovering from trauma is a long and complex road—unique to each individual. Even though you can't fix the main problem, I urge you to focus on the little things—because they do matter.

Having said that, even the little things may be met with resistance. Your loved one might be struggling internally to control their emotions. They'll resist because they don't want to be a burden. They'll resist because they don't want to be judged. They'll resist because they're feeling erratic, out of control, and they don't want to draw attention to their recovery process, wherever they may be.

During my recovery, I didn't want to be treated differently, because that would have made me feel like I was damaged. I thus resisted a lot of help that was offered. Thankfully, my family and friends didn't let me stop them. Their help didn't always look like "help," either. They weren't trying to be obvious with their efforts. In fact, the best help doesn't look like help at all. It comes across as casual, like the gesture is no big deal.

If their first response is a no, ask again later. Ask again later that day, or later that week. Your loved one may push you away again, but don't give up. Persist. Offer your unconditional support. When appropriate, despite the resistance, go ahead and do it anyway. Do their laundry. Bring them pizza. Take them on their favorite hike (if they can handle it). Get them out of the house for some fresh air. Even a drive around town listening to some music helped me feel better. When you get through to them, the little comforts you provide make a *huge* difference. Homemade chicken pot pie delivered by a friend and fleece sheets to tuck myself into at night made me so happy after my surgery, even if they didn't change my medical situation. They provided me with a little comfort that seemed to ease the pain my body was feeling.

The trick is figuring out which little things are needed and when, because the healing process is always evolving. Your loved one might not be able to tell you exactly what they need, but it never hurts to ask. They might be able to tell you if something is helpful, or if another approach would be better. Take it upon yourself to get creative and see how you can help. Read between the lines. Don't be afraid to get specific and tailor your approach to your loved one's personality; you know them best.

Everyone is different, but here are some questions to help get you started:

- Are there any household chores I can do to help their living situation? Is there a constant pile of dishes in the sink? Can I do their laundry? Can I vacuum their house once a week? Can I help them get things organized? This would be particularly helpful to those who like to keep their homes tidy but are overwhelmed or struggling with motivation due to their trauma.
- Is my loved one eating? Can I bring dinner over? Can I have a pizza delivered to their house? Can I make their favorite dessert? Can I take them out for ice cream?
- Are they overwhelmed with the medical world? Can I research doctors or therapists for them? Can I suggest someone I know and trust? Can I take them to their appointments for support?
- How is their mobility? Can they drive? Do they need a ride to a medical appointment? Do they need a ride to a family member's or friend's house?
- How can I meet them where they're at? How can I spend quality time with them? I know this is broad, but it doesn't have to be complicated. A friend of mine would come over and we'd play a different board game each week. Video games were too stimulating for me. Think of something that isn't incredibly demanding on them, but enough to lift their spirits. Watch a movie or a TV show together—and don't forget to pop some popcorn for sharing. Most of the time just having someone around can provide an incredible amount of comfort.

My mother kept nudging me, asking me to do little things with her. We'd go for a ride just to get out of the house, or go grab some ice cream. We ate dinner together in the evening and binge-watched *Hell's Kitchen* and *New Amsterdam* at night. That meant everything to me, because it was calm, I felt safe, and I didn't feel like a burden. I just felt supported. My mom just took it upon herself to do things that she thought would bring some happiness into my life—and they did.

You have to take the initiative, because your loved one may never reach out on their own. It's common for trauma victims to isolate themselves because they often feel that no one understands what they are going through, and sharing their thoughts and feelings will lead to judgments. Be conscious of that, and be extra sensitive to them. If they do share their thoughts and feelings with you, keep an open mind and heart. Don't question what they are feeling or why they are feeling that way. Just listen to what they are saying.

And don't forget to give them a big hug afterward (if they're open to that).

TRY, TRY AGAIN

I'm especially grateful to those who kept asking, even after I rudely dismissed them. They knew that an offer rejected in week one might be welcomed in week five, because the process unfolds over time; no two days in recovery are ever the same.

Not everyone realizes this. Most people assume that recovery is a constant upward progression: the person is injured, gets a diagnosis, follows the doctor's orders, and gets better. If only it were that easy! In reality, the path of recovery is filled with unexpected obstacles and degrees of suffering the patient may not understand, or even recognize.

I couldn't acknowledge I suffered from PTSD for a long time. The time I spent immersed in the chaotic corrections system kept me from processing my experience as trauma. I thought that if you were strong-willed enough, you'd be immune to it, and I wasn't going to let it get me.

Once I was out of that environment, I had trouble adjusting to my new normal. After nine months of trauma therapy, I was still jumping out of my seat when someone threw their coffee cup in their trash can at work. I couldn't handle people raising their voices or being confrontational. If a certain song came on the radio, it would trigger memories to ugly incidents at the jail. Reading newspaper articles about former residents also gave me horrible flashbacks of all the various hardships I endured in the high-risk unit. I didn't acknowledge that those were all symptoms of PTSD. When I initially saw the DSM criteria in black and white, I didn't think it applied to me, but if I go back to it now, there's no doubt.

Negative emotional state? Check.

Feeling detached? Check.

Unable to experience positive emotions? Check.

Heightened startle response, difficulty concentrating, problems sleeping? Check, check, check.

It couldn't have been more obvious, but I didn't see it until a month after my surgery. Even though things were so much better without those insufferable migraines, I still had a lot of the same problems. I'd been downplaying my trauma, brushing it off as no big deal, but one day, just puttering around the house, I suddenly understood it was a *huge* deal! One look in the mirror gave me plenty of hard evidence to prove the case: I could see stitches running from ear to ear and a gaping wound on my head. Someone had done an awful lot of damage to me. It took me a very long time to fully accept that I wasn't invincible after all.

It's safe to say I was *much* more responsive to offers of help once the denial lifted and I could acknowledge that I was victimized, vulnerable, and unable to control everything in my world. Only then could I recognize the PTSD piece and begin to talk about it to others, which was an incredible help.

But it took two years for me to get there.

Your loved one will react differently at different stages, too, so if they reject your offer, they're just not ready. Meet them where they are at, and try again later. If you're patient and stick around, you can be there when your loved one is ready to accept your help.

THINGS TO REMEMBER WHEN LOVING SOMEONE WITH DEPRESSION

Lessons Learned in Life, a motivational website about life, published an article titled, "7 Things to Remember When You Love Someone with Depression,"* which was spot-on in their advice, so I wanted to highlight their list in hopes that it will help you. I recommend reading the article in its entirety, as it goes into greater detail about each point.

1. They're not choosing to be depressed.
2. Being there for them in whatever way they need you is the best thing that you can do.
3. It's okay for you to feel frustrated.
4. How people treat you is a reflection of how they feel about themselves, rather than how they feel about you.
5. Discussing and setting boundaries is important.
6. People with depression can become easily over-whelmed.
7. It's not about you.

---

* https://lessonslearnedinlife.com/
7-things-to-remember-when-you-love-a-person-who-has-depression/

MEDICAL PERSONNEL

As I've clawed my way back to health, I've had some fantastic interactions with doctors, nurses, and other medical personnel. Many providers, like Donna and Maureen, went above and beyond the call of duty, but others did the bare minimum and sent me on my way. I've also had plenty of office visits that were, at best, a waste of my time. At worst, I'd leave feeling worse than when I went in.

I know that was never anyone's intention. I know people working in medicine are there because they want to help their patients, but sometimes they need to be reminded of how the medical system feels to the patient. To that end, I've developed a list of things I wish my medical providers had done, but didn't always.

My wish list for medical providers:

1. Listen to your patient, because no matter how much you know about how brain injuries are "supposed to" present, each situation is unique. My trajectory was longer than most, and I often felt like doctors just wanted to be done with me. They seemed offended that my thick medical file and I were in their office again, when, in their mind, I should have been healed by six months, or a year, or certainly eighteen months.

2. Think beyond the standard protocol, if necessary. Doctors should have a menu of alternative options to offer when they haven't gotten positive results with their usual repertoire. Patients need hope; even if you can't help them, maybe you can refer them to someone who

can, or at least give them a next thing to try. When a doctor handed me cards for a craniosacral therapist and a massage therapist after telling me there was nothing he could do for me, he was handing me hope.

3. Give your patients the full story. Keep up-to-date on the research and explain the best currently available evidence to your patient. It's hard for the patient to know whom to trust when they get conflicting advice, like I did at first. One doctor said it was imperative to sit in the dark to recover from a concussion, while another one told me the sooner a person gets back to functioning, the sooner their brain recovers.

4. Be like Donna. Believe in your patients 100 percent, and advocate for them when they can't do it themselves. When Donna took over, she took the reins and set me up for the appointments I needed. It felt foreign to have someone else so invested in my life, but it was also a relief to feel like someone cared enough to take care of me. Before Donna, nobody looked at the whole picture of my recovery and took the initiative to do what I couldn't do for myself. Her perseverance was the key to turning my situation around.

PUT PEOPLE FIRST

Preventing a workplace injury in fields like law enforcement, corrections, firefighting, military, and other front-line occupations is an impossibility, but how the workplace treats their injured workers can have a significant impact on their recovery—for the good or bad.

Employers can attempt to mitigate workplace injuries by establishing appropriate policies regarding various situations. Unfortunately, the individuals who write the policies and the individuals whom the policies affect are usually two different groups.

In my situation, most of the administrators who were responsible for establishing our daily policies and procedures never stepped foot inside our secure perimeter, let alone saw firsthand the events that took place. These administrators had different priorities that didn't involve those who worked on the front line. While *they* cared about their public image, statistics, and grant money, *we* cared about keeping ourselves, other staff, and inmates safe. The policies that were implemented to further the administration's goals in reality made the facility a much more dangerous environment for both staff and inmates.

Working in these types of careers can be incredibly demanding, demoralizing, and damaging to individuals. It is critical for employers to value their employees for the tireless work they do (which often went unnoticed). From my own experience, no people in the building—not inmates, not staff—were treated like humans with hopes, dreams, and brains by our administration. We were not people; we were just a part of the internal workings of the building. Each day, our mission was to make sure nobody died and the facility didn't get sued. That was it. It didn't matter if we had just been forced to work overtime twice already this week; we were getting forced again today. We weren't individuals; we were warm bodies needed to staff positions. Unfortunately, this is the status quo for most detention facilities across the country, so my experience with one such facility is not unique.

Few administrators at the jail expressed compassion, which frustrated us to no end. If we had a night on the unit when one staff member got a concussion, another a split eye, and a third a broken nose, nobody would even ask about their well-being, or try to figure out how to prevent it from happening again. The only questions that mattered were: Did it look bad on camera? Did we act within policy? How soon can you have that report up? That was it.

Until I started working at the revenue office, I didn't fully realize how vulnerable we really were at the detention center. I knew the work was dangerous, but the supervisors who worked on the floor had my back. The administrators setting the policies, however, were on another page entirely and were happy just to hang us out to dry.

In my new job, it feels like everybody is on the same team, up and down the chain of command. My work gets reviewed by senior management, which is amazing because we have the same goals: holding people accountable, doing the right thing, and making sure our work means something.

Back at the detention center, interaction with senior administrators was limited to a quick nod at the annual Employee Appreciation Day. At my new office, the division director comes to our Christmas party and gives us all handwritten notes and a small gift. Of course, it's not a perfect environment, but we feel like we're all in it together. If an employer is interested in creating a culture where their people feel respected, appreciated, and heard, there are small gestures they can do that can leave a lasting impression on their employees.

Would a proactive, team-based work culture have prevented my assault? There's no way of knowing, but if my coworkers and I were able to advocate and share opinions when it came to establishing policies and procedures, that day might have turned out very differently. This could have been easily achieved by offering open discussions with the administrators during shift briefings a few times during the year. We would have felt like our voices were heard, and maybe the administration would get a better idea of what their "policies" actually look like when they are put into place.

But alas, these things are no longer in my purview—which is a good thing.

CONCLUSION

Before starting my new job in October 2017, four months after my assault, I went back to the detention center to return my uniform. While I was there catching up with old coworkers, my unit manager asked if I would speak with my assailant. "Sure," I said. "Absolutely."

We've always promoted conflict resolution at the jail, encouraging the inmates to talk things out, whether that was between inmates, with staff members, or in their personal life. My guess was that the unit manager approached him and told him that I would be coming in that day, and he would have the opportunity to meet with me, if he wanted. Turned out he did. The inmate and I met in my supervisor's small office, so there were three of us at the table.

As much as I wanted to come across as the bigger person,

and as a strong individual for confronting my assailant for the first time since the assault, my emotions were mixed. I was angry, and I would be lying if I didn't say that I felt slightly nervous walking into this small back office. The only reason I agreed to sit down with this individual was because I hoped he would take something from it that would make a difference at some point in his life.

I entered the room and sat down across from him. "I'm sorry," my assailant said to me. "It was you or me, you know?"

I knew; I knew all along. I saw the hand this kid was dealt in life, and in that moment he didn't have many choices. He was scared of the older inmate—much more scared than he was of me. Pair that fear with low impulse control and no place to run, and the assault was almost inevitable.

"I forgive you," I told him. "I just hope you can start making better decisions moving forward."

I'm grateful I had the opportunity to meet with him. I wanted him to know I didn't blame him. He was a very emotional and sensitive person who faced a lot of loss in his life, and although he should still take responsibility for his actions, I understood that prison culture often led young people to make unwise decisions.

A DISAPPOINTING SENTENCING

Before my assailant's sentencing for my assault, I received a call from the district attorney. "I'd like to drop the charge for this inmate's assault on you from a Class C felony to a misdemeanor," she said. Although the charge was brought on by the state, as the victim, they contacted me for my input on the matter.

"Absolutely not," I told her. I was utterly offended that those words even came out of her mouth. An assault on an officer is generally classified as a Class C felony. "He's assaulted six other staff members since I left," I continued. "Thankfully, none of those attacks were as severe as mine, but that's not the point. Do *not* drop or reduce his charge."

Even though I forgave what he did to me, he still needed to be held accountable for his actions. And swinging deals was the cause of my assault in the first place, so I was adamant about not budging.

On top of that, I knew all the other assault charges against him would be dropped to misdemeanors. Since officers get assaulted so frequently at our juvenile facility, the DAs usually drop the majority of the assault charges. At adult prisons, on the other hand, if an inmate hits an officer, they get three to five years—regardless of whether the inmate missed his punch or drew blood. With juveniles, however, unless they break a nose or cause significant damage, they likely won't be charged at all. The charges in my case, therefore, were the only ones severe enough to be classified as a felony, so there was no way in hell I was going to agree to reduce them.

It all boiled down to politics and bureaucracy. State officials didn't want their state to come across as if it wasn't giving these juveniles a chance. They didn't want the public to think they're hard on juveniles, making it even harder for them to turn their lives around. So they coddled them and continually gave them chance, after chance, after chance. And since the inmates had such a long history of avoiding consequences, they'd take advantage of the system. During my time there, the state ran a report that compared statistics across all of their facilities. The total number of assaults on staff members at my facility were at least five times higher than all the adult facilities in the entire state—combined! For inmates, it was like open season on staff, knowing that most assault charges would be dropped. We were not aggressive enough with our legal system when it came to juveniles.

My assailant's sentencing was scheduled for December 2017, five months after the assault. Since what happened the night of the assault was much more complicated than simply an inmate attacking an officer—and despite the lawyers already agreeing on the sentence—I felt compelled to speak and share my story.

"This assault caused me five months of constant pain and suffering, multiple trips to the hospital, dozens of doctors, PT, and therapy appointments," I told those in attendance. Since this was a juvenile case, it was confidential, so the only people in the room were the lawyers from each side, the judge, my victim advocate, the inmate, and myself.

"No sentence will return to me what he has taken away," I continued. "He single-handedly destroyed my life and left me to piece it back together. Having that said, I don't have any animosity toward this young man. I've looked out for him. I helped him with his homework. He confided in me. Unfortunately, he was forced into a bad situation because of a deal made by people similar to those here today."

Reading from the pages of notes I gripped in my hands, I told them that the corrections system was broken. Their lenient policies against violent juvenile offenders were not helping them—referring to the Pod Father, the inmate who was allowed back into the juvenile facility after escaping. "The criminal justice system failed by allowing this dangerous criminal to return to a juvenile facility, after committing a felony as an adult. Dangerous individuals over the age of eighteen do not belong here, as they manipulate young, vulnerable residents and turn them into more sophisticated criminals."

I also told them that the broken system had broken me. My agonizing pain, my unrelenting migraines (which were happening while I spoke), and the times I'd lost my will to live all happened because Pod Father was in a place he didn't belong. When I met with my assailant a couple of months before, we didn't talk about the pain I was in, or the damage that he'd caused, so this information was all new to him. He didn't look at me once while I spoke.

"There is no justice for me here today," I concluded. "I can only hope that you take the appropriate steps to keep this from happening to someone else. My assault could have been prevented, but the criminal justice system failed me."

Speaking my piece didn't change the system, but it was healing for me to speak the truth at last. My hope was that maybe those in the room would think twice before cutting anymore deals with juveniles in the future.

After I spoke, it was time to hear the final sentencing. The judge read off more than a half-dozen charges, to which the inmate pleaded guilty to. The misdemeanor charges from him assaulting other officers were bundled in with my felony charge. With the damage he did and with his history of violent outbursts, I expected him to get a bind over, which meant he would start accruing adult time for any additional charges moving forward. In other words, he would start getting charged as an adult.

Instead, the inmate only got an additional six months added

to his juvenile sentence. My entire chest tightened. *Six months? That's it?* It was an absolute slap in the face.

They did it because they didn't want to keep him in the juvenile system any longer. Because I refused to lessen the charges, they had to give him *some* time, but they didn't want to add *too much* time, since they wanted him out.

I was angry for a long time after, because I felt like my life was stolen and there was nothing I could do about it. Back then, I was struggling to reach a baseline level of health, so that's what I focused on.

The young man who assaulted me has since been released back into society. The one who orchestrated my attack was still in jail, albeit at another adult facility. Two years after my assault, however, I stopped following up on my previous inmates. Ignorance is bliss, and I just prefer not to know anymore.

LIFE TODAY

Even as my assault broke me down, it provided unexpected clarity as to how I approached life. Before the attack, I was ambitious and accomplished, but I was also pretty unhappy and angry. I was always running toward the next goal, not because I felt good about it, but because I thought I had something to prove to the world. And surely, if I just got the next job or the next degree, I'd be happy. I was so busy meeting self-imposed deadlines that I never learned to be happy with myself as I was.

The recovery process stripped all of that away. I have learned to be open to a different level of love, trust, and support from the people around me, people who loved me even when my biggest accomplishment was getting out of bed each day. And I've learned to love myself on those days, too. I'm not as hard on myself as I used to be, nor do I hold myself up to unrealistic standards.

I now know I can't control every outcome, and, paradoxically, letting go of control has led to some of the best outcomes in my life. I have a great job, I bought a house, and I live near my family. I'm content in my life and more compassionate toward others, feelings I rarely experienced when I was running headlong at external goals.

Through my therapy sessions, and through my cats, I quelled the anxiety I had regarding downtime. Everyone always told me to work less and take more time for myself, so I finally listened and started working only one job. Focusing my energies on only one job opened up more time to focus on myself, my goals, and the things I love to do. One of those goals was to complete a doctoral program, so that's what I ended up doing. I was unsure if my brain injury would keep me from completing my master's, but once I earned it, I felt like I couldn't stop. Education has always been something I valued, so I'm currently pursuing a doctorate degree in business administration.

I haven't had a single migraine since my surgery. My head is still numb, but only on the left side where they removed the nerve, so when I brush my hair, I can't feel anything in that area.

I meet with Maureen once a month to continue working through PTSD. Donna checks in with me every two weeks to see how I'm doing. I still have gut-wrenching nightmares that leave me drenched in my own sweat. I often wake up thinking people are in my house, for example. My nightmares are still as real as ever, emotionally and physically draining, so much so that around the three-year anniversary of my assault, I reached my limit. I was curious to find out if there was an expert I could see who could layer on top of my therapy in hopes that I could do something more for the nightmares to eventually go away.

My primary health practitioner suggested I get a sleep study. I didn't anticipate anything to come out of it. I only did it to see if it would lead me to an expert who could help me. In fact, several people told me that I shouldn't do it, that it would be a waste of time. "They only check for sleep apnea or restless leg syndrome, Derryen," they'd say. "These sleep studies don't address nightmares."

I wasn't a candidate for either of those diagnoses. But if there's anything I've learned throughout my journey, it's to keep an open mind and leave no stone unturned, so I went ahead and did it. A week later, they called me to inform me of my results. "You are suffering from central sleep apnea. Your study showed that you stopped breathing when you sleep. In fact, you stopped breathing about every six minutes."

I was surprised by the news, but was interested in hearing about the next steps to address it. "So, something's physically blocking my ability to breathe at night?" I asked.

"No," the woman on the phone responded. "Your brain is no longer sending signals to your diaphragm to get you to breathe when you are sleeping."

There are two types of sleep apnea. There's the sleep apnea with a physical obstruction—usually caused by a crooked nose, large tonsils, excess weight, etc.—that blocks the ability to breathe. And then there's central apnea, the one I have, which is found in people who have endured traumatic brain injuries. In fact, one-third of those with traumatic brain injuries suffer from sleep apnea, but people (medical professionals included) just don't associate the two.

In order for my body to start breathing again, it dumps adrenaline and stress hormones into my system to get me to wake up and breathe. When I stop breathing, my brain thinks I'm dying, so in order to wake me up, my dreams have to be intense enough to jolt me awake so my diaphragm starts working again.

So I sleep with a breathing machine now, a CPAP. There is no cure. There is nothing I can do to address or improve the condition, either. And I am bound to use a breathing machine for the rest of my life at twenty-six years old.

I was devastated at first. I have to sleep with a breathing machine for the rest of my life? How am I going to find a partner? Navigating this world is challenging enough, and now I have yet another disability to deal with? It was a lot to take in.

And yet, at the same time, I got answers. There *was* more to my night terrors than I thought. My exhausting and horrific nightmares served a purpose: they kept me alive. Even though there was nothing I could do to fix the sleep apnea, I was being proactive. Maybe the breathing machine would help. Maybe I wouldn't be so tired all the time.

It's still early, but after the first month of using the CPAP, my nightmares have been less violent, and I have felt more rested. Some days are better than others, but it's a start.

None of my doctors on my journey recommended a sleep

study, but that's probably because I didn't present with the common risk factors for sleep apnea, like being overweight or having throat issues. It just goes to show that even if you're not a poster child for a disorder, brain injuries are a totally different animal, so you should be open to all sorts of tests.

I'm still working as a revenue agent for the state. I'm a principal agent now, which means more responsibility, like training new agents, and a little more independence. I get to choose my own cases, which I find super motivating. I'm no longer bothered by working in a cubicle. A desk job is obviously less stressful than working in a detention center. One of my favorite aspects of this job is the consistency. Expectations don't change, and I'm not as dependent on others to do my work.

I still keep in contact with some of my old coworkers from the jail (including my supervisor, whom I adore—we've even enjoyed some fishing excursions together!), but from what I hear from them, things haven't changed over there. Politics is still the main driver behind all decisions, not the well-being of the kids or the staff.

Without debilitating migraines, one of the things I've most looked forward to is being active again. I recently signed up for a dance class and an intramural sports league once a week and am looking forward to hiking in the summers.

Most of all, I look forward to enjoying life again. I was consumed with finding the answer to my migraines for two years. Even when I tried doing something fun, the migraines ruined it. I tried to live in the moment, to be present, to enjoy those around me or my surroundings, but the migraines were too distracting. Everything was miserable. Now, I can finally live my life—and I have a whole new checklist in my mind:

Enjoy owning my own home, check.

Spend quality time with my family, check.

Cuddling with my cats, Kanga and Roo, check.

Reaching out to others who share similar experiences, in progress.

LOOKING FORWARD: HELPING OTHERS

I couldn't get to where I am until I learned to articulate my pain and express my needs. This book has been part of that process, and it's been very healing for me, but I also wrote it to help others feel less alone.

I know how much of a difference it made to watch a simple online video of a brain-injury patient talking about losing her depth perception. She traced her way down every step as I did! What a relief to realize I wasn't alone. I hope my story provides the same kind of respite for others, and I've been working on reaching out to others who may be suffering from PTSD, brain injuries, vision loss, and so forth.

Just recently, I spoke with a woman who had reservations about the same occipital neuralgia surgery I went through. This woman's experience was very similar to mine. She sustained a brain injury on the job, was suffering from severe migraines that didn't change throughout the day, and felt incredibly frustrated living in constant pain with no answers.

"I've been suffering from these intense migraines for the past year," she told me over the phone, "but I'm super nervous about the surgery." We connected over how isolating and irritable the migraines made us, how alone we felt in our struggles, and how it changed our personalities.

"This is not who I am," she said. "I don't even want to tell anyone what I'm dealing with because they just don't understand."

"I know exactly what you're talking about," I told her. "I know how you're feeling. It's absolutely miserable, nobody gets it, and everything sucks."

"Surgery is my last option. What if it works? What if it doesn't? It's a scary place to be in."

"For sure," I said. "I can't promise that everything's going to be all right, but the surgery did work for me, so it may work for you. But one thing is for certain, if you don't try, it's guaranteed not to get better, so at least trying gives you a chance."

By the end our conversation, she felt better. "You've given me hope," she told me. "Thank you."

With a new lease on life, I want to pay it forward. From the broken pieces, I want to create something beautiful. I don't know what that looks like just yet, but I want to help others. Maybe that's being a voice for brain injuries, for trauma, or for PTSD. Maybe it's getting involved with groups to reduce the stigma of brain injuries and PTSD. Different states are starting to enact legislation to provide additional resources to first responders to help them through things like PTSD; maybe I could be a part of that. All I know is that I want to support those who are going through what I went through. I want to let them know they are not alone.

Whatever it is, I want to make a difference.

Follow along with me on this journey at www.derryenplante. com.

ACKNOWLEDGMENTS

Openly writing and sharing my experiences surrounding the most difficult events of my life was harder and more healing than I could have ever imagined. I wouldn't have made it to this point without the incredible people who have been by my side through these ordeals.

I am beyond thankful for my parents, who provided me with the initial support I needed to continue to seek answers and start my fight to take my life back. Thank you for your unconditional love, encouragement, and understanding through it all. I love you.

I'm eternally grateful to my case manager, Donna, who took the reins, left no stone unturned, and was determined to see me get better. If there was a mountain, you would have moved an entire range of them if it meant improving my health. You were the first person who truly heard what I was saying, believed me wholeheartedly, and made me feel like I wasn't in this fight alone. I owe my recovery to you. Thank you for being my biggest advocate.

I could not have gotten to this point without my confidant, Maureen, who has worked with me through the good, the bad, and the ugly. You have been by my side through the denial, and now through the processing. From the times I didn't want to talk, or couldn't find the words, your support was unwavering when I needed it most. Thank you.

My best friend, Sarah, who has seen me through the worst times: you always offered an ear to listen or a shoulder to cry on. Even when I was trying my best to put on a good face, you always saw through it and never shied away from giving comfort or support. Thank you for standing by me through all my struggles. You are an amazing friend.

I could not be more thankful for those individuals who have supported me throughout my journey to get me to where I am today. To Michael Maloney, the first person who ever fully believed that I could accomplish the big dreams I set for myself: it is because of your belief in me that I have not lost faith in myself. To Mr. J: you always had my back and supported me when no one else would.

To those who have assisted in my journey, friends, coworkers, medical providers: thank you. Each one of you has had a significant impact on how I navigated my way through my recovery.

Although this period of my life was filled with many ups and downs, I am appreciative of the opportunity to share my life through this book. Writing a book about such a traumatic life event is an incredibly profound process. This could not have been accomplished without Aleks Mendel, Maggie Rains, and Sheila Trask. Thank you for your editorial help, keen insight, and compassionate support in bringing my stories to these pages. Without you and the team at Scribe, I could not have shared my story.

ABOUT THE AUTHOR

DERRYEN PLANTE is a survivor who battled back from a traumatic brain injury and redefined herself in the wake of a horrific attack that altered the course of her life.

Derryen received her BS from St. Lawrence University in 2015 (mathematics-economics combined and psychology), her master's degree in criminal justice from Boston University in 2019, and is currently working on her doctorate degree in business administration from Northcentral University. She currently works as a principal revenue agent for the State of Maine, where she resides with her two adorable cats, Kanga and Roo.

She wrote this book to create a connection with others suffering with an invisible injury and to offer them strength to build a new life post-injury. From the broken pieces, she was able to create something beautiful. She hopes she can inspire others to do the same.

To further connect with Derryen, visit DerryenPlante.com.